# SMART CITIES

**The MIT Press Essential Knowledge Series**

A complete list of the titles in this series appears at the back of the book.

# SMART CITIES

GERMAINE R. HALEGOUA

The MIT Press | Cambridge, Massachusetts | London, England

This book was set in Chaparral Pro by Toppan Best-set Premedia Limited. Printed and bound in the United States of America.

Library of Congress Cataloging-in-Publication Data

Names: Halegoua, Germaine R., 1979- author.
Title: Smart cities / Germaine R. Halegoua.
Description: Cambridge, MA : MIT Press, [2020] | Series: MIT Press essential knowledge series | Includes bibliographical references and index.
Identifiers: LCCN 2019015278 | ISBN 9780262538053 (pbk. : alk. paper)
Subjects: LCSH: Smart cities. | Cities and towns—Effect of technological innovations on.
Classification: LCC TD159.4 .H35 2020 | DDC 307.760285—dc23
LC record available at https://lccn.loc.gov/2019015278

10   9   8   7   6   5   4   3   2   1

# CONTENTS

# SERIES FOREWORD

The MIT Press Essential Knowledge series offers accessible, concise, beautifully produced pocket-size books on topics of current interest. Written by leading thinkers, the books in this series deliver expert overviews of subjects that range from the cultural and the historical to the scientific and the technical.

In today's era of instant information gratification, we have ready access to opinions, rationalizations, and superficial descriptions. Much harder to come by is the foundational knowledge that informs a principled understanding of the world. Essential Knowledge books fill that need. Synthesizing specialized subject matter for nonspecialists and engaging critical topics through fundamentals, each of these compact volumes offers readers a point of access to complex ideas.

*Bruce Tidor*
*Professor of Biological Engineering and Computer Science*
*Massachusetts Institute of Technology*

Journalists as well as municipal officials have been eager to declare certain cities to be the first, largest, or most innovative "smart city" in the world. For example, on January 1, 2017, the technology news website *Digital Trends* listed Singapore, Barcelona, Oslo, and New York City as four cities that have integrated "the most cutting-edge smart technologies" and "never-before-tested city planning initiatives" into urban space and urban life. Among these innovations were ubiquitous sensors, cameras, and Wi-Fi networks used to monitor and report traffic flows, energy and water consumption, and crime in domestic and public spaces, along with the automation of mundane aspects of everyday life—from the programmed illumination of streetlights to sensors that count toilet flushes. Uniting these cities under the category of "smart" are goals of improving "urban problems" through digital technology "solutions." By accumulating and processing digital information about certain urban activities, mobilities, and infrastructures, smart city developers hope to make cities more responsive, efficient, sustainable, and safe.

Urban environments promoted as "smart cities" have become both crucibles and showrooms for the practical application of the Internet of things (IoT), cloud computing, and the integration of big data processing into everyday life. Over the past 10 years, technology companies, governments, and urban developers all over the world have promoted smart cities as attainable future places where urban life is made knowable and manageable through data collection and analysis. These urban spaces are imagined as utilizing enhanced digital infrastructure, real-time data, and ubiquitous computing to foster efficiency in city management and governance and to improve quality of life for urban residents. Cities that are not yet "smart" are recognized as inefficient spaces; they may utilize technology to function but might be using outdated infrastructure and network models or collecting data about some, but not all, urban activities.

Government agencies, technology companies, and independent foundations have offered competitive funding opportunities with names like "Smart Cities Challenge" and "Smart Gigabit Communities Program" to encourage smart city construction. Public-private partnerships between municipal or national governments and corporations such as Cisco, IBM, Intel, Microsoft, and Siemens have produced plans to retrofit existing cities with sensors, digital kiosks, public Wi-Fi, and Internet-ready cameras, and to build new smart cities from the ground up. Although smart cities are being discussed and constructed worldwide, there is limited consensus about the concept, purpose, and consequences surrounding smart city development.

Are smart cities disruptive, or even innovative, urban developments? As more cities that claim to be smart are built or retrofitted across the globe, debates on this question have proliferated. Proponents of smart city development emphasize the role of technology in "smart growth," improved public services, efficient infrastructures, and entrepreneurial competitiveness. However, critics voice suspicion about the datafication of urban processes, surveillance of urban populations, and the eagerness of public officials to regard information and communication technologies (ICTs) as "solutions" for perceived urban problems. Still other researchers and planners see great potential in smart city enterprises that broaden ideas about data collection and use, include input from urban residents, and foster collaboration with communities and neighborhoods.

The corporate- or technology-driven iterations of the smart city are only a subset of many possible ways that urban informatics can take hold, but they currently remain the dominant model for smart city development. Several critics note the ways in which these visions of the connected or networked city are highly problematic. For example, the city is not merely a series of technological solutions that process or optimize urban life; it is an actually existing place where lived experiences and preexisting community behaviors should be understood and integrated into urban infrastructures. Emergent smart city planning and goals have begun to shift conversations and innovations away from the indiscriminate implementation of sensors and IoT for efficiency and optimization, toward socially and culturally informed understandings of urban issues and inequities, an expanded roster of smart city stakeholders and policymakers, and the use of big data for public benefit. Questions linger about whom the smart city is for, how to measure its success, and who participates in its creation and use; they should continue to be asked of the companies and government entities that support these projects and the agencies that fund smart city development.

As the concerns and potential promises of smart cities multiply, it is imperative that citizens and scholars understand the processes and issues at hand. Many discussions and policy decisions about smart cities occur within boardrooms or conferences geared toward technology industry representatives, government officials, and urban developers. In order for members of the public to contribute to the development of urban space, they will need to understand the urban transformations being proposed, how their cities and towns are being reshaped by digital media implementation and use, and where and how they can intervene in these processes.

Since 2009, I have studied both smart-from-the-start and retrofitted cities that adopt or plan to adopt government-mandated or corporate models of smart city development (e.g., Songdo and Kansas City), and the social inequities and tensions that arise from doing so. In researching these relationships, I have interviewed representatives from Cisco and Google and have attended city cabinet meetings and smart city conferences and events in order to analyze the values, visions, and social decisions around corporate smart city models. I have also observed and interviewed digital inclusion activists, neighborhood organizers, and people who have never had Internet access and feel entirely excluded from smart city visions and/or do not know enough about the concepts, vocabulary, and politics to question or offer alternatives to these endeavors.

In this book, I interrogate corporate visions of smart city development because they tend to be the model that is the most common and least understood or questioned by nonspecialist audiences as well as by many of the municipal officials who adopt it. Although corporate imaginations have dominated discourse on smart city development, there are alternative ways of thinking about what the smart city is and whom it is for. Throughout this book I introduce some alternative forms and perspectives on smart city development that have taken shape in cities around the world.

Dominant discourses about the smart city tend to present "smart" as an end goal for urban development and urban living without adequately explaining or interrogating the meaning, processes, or politics behind this trajectory. I wanted to write this book because I am troubled by the fact that the corporate model of smart city development has become canonical and the role of corporations in the design of smart cities continues to deepen. I have written about unchecked corporate visions of smart cities in terms of limited opportunities for citizen engagement and collaboration, myopic visions of technological futures, and failures to imagine the city as a diverse, inhabited place. I am equally troubled every time I witness chief information officers (CIOs) and chief executive officers (CEOs) ward off citizen concerns about surveillance, privacy, and social justice issues with perfunctory or elusive answers that are laden with jargon or promissory rhetoric about big data and improved quality of life. However, there are plenty of opportunities to create socially just smart cities, and many people within planning departments, universities, grassroots organizations, neighborhood collectives, and energy, communication, and computing industries are actively working to do so. Increasingly, some smart city advocates are beginning to consider the uneven effects of ICT implementation on marginalized populations, and are developing ways to educate and include diverse stakeholders in smart city plans. By focusing on corporate models, I do not intend to espouse or amplify engineered, profit-driven visions of smart city development at the expense of more citizen-focused imaginations. Instead, I aim to familiarize specialists and nonspecialists with the rhetorical processes and promises used to support corporate ideologies in order to open informed social, political, and ethical critiques of the same, and to present alternative ways of thinking about data and ICTs in urban space.

This book will contextualize and assess the concept of the smart city through an evaluation of materials from popular, industry, and scholarly work as well as my own fieldwork. Each chapter includes a range of arguments against the smart city as well as examples of selective use of technologies to meet policy goals and citizen needs for sustainable, responsive, accessible, or engaged cities. One of the aims of the book is to identify and discuss competing visions of what is at stake in building and managing smart cities. In particular, I juxtapose arguments for smart cities as optimized, sustainable, digitally networked solutions to urban problems that improve quality of life against critiques of smart cities as neoliberal, corporate-controlled, undemocratic non-places. By introducing concepts, definitions, specific examples, and historical contexts for smart cities, this book equips readers with some background to engage in current conversations and debates on the present and future of smart city development. The book provides some of the literacy needed to recognize the limits of technological "smartness" as an urban goal through examples of canonic and emerging business plans and development models (chapter 2), an evaluation of technology use (chapter 3), and citizen input and engagement within smart city endeavors (chapter 4).

The book begins with a review of key definitions and terminology utilized by urban planners and developers, technology designers, journalists, and researchers. Chapter 1 outlines some justifications for smart city development and promises of digital media in current smart city planning and implementation. Chapter 2 highlights three overarching models in the development of smart cities and presents a brief survey of established and emerging business and network management plans in a variety of cities. Chapter 3 introduces key technologies and methods currently in use or under development for gathering and analyzing data about urban environments. Chapter 4 draws on fieldwork and documentation of how smart city developers conceive of interactions between the built environment, technological and urban infrastructures, and citizen engagement. Chapter 5 summarizes current perspectives and key takeaways presented in previous chapters and discusses emerging perspectives and themes in regard to smart city development and research.

Throughout this book I argue that smart city developers need to work more closely with local communities to understand their preexisting relationships to urban place and realize the limits of technological fixes. If municipal governments want to utilize digital technologies to improve quality of life for all, then technology deployment must be viewed as a means to an end instead of an end itself. Citizens and urban communities need to play a larger role in defining the end to which those technologies will be put. However, city governments, smart city developers, and urban residents don't always know how to have these conversations or how to encourage people to define how and under what conditions technologies and data will be employed. In the concluding chapter, I will suggest some preliminary ways to do so.

Local communities need more information about how smart cities are being conceived and implemented in order to intervene in decisions about smart city development. We need more citizens, more diverse populations with intimate knowledge about what it means and feels like to live in cities, and more people who care about equitable access to technology, data, and city services to be part of the conversations that shape what smart cities will become. I hope this book will help to propel this process.

# AN INTRODUCTION TO SMART CITIES

Facing myriad definitions and mission statements offering promissory yet vague descriptions of innovative urban environments, scholars use the term "nebulous" to describe the contemporary smart city. However, there are common characteristics and goals in these seemingly imprecise descriptions. Although heralded as new and innovative, smart city discourses, technologies, and administrative practices can be contextualized within longer histories of city management and the use of ICTs within urban space. Smart cities raise new incarnations of recurring, fundamental questions about city management: who governs, how, and what aspects of the city are governable? How can cities be planned to create communities, manage growth, and effectively distribute resources and services? Governance and city management are never easy, and technical aids have been employed by planners, administrators, and residents for centuries to organize urban complexity. In this vein, municipal governments are lured by ideals of simplicity and order that computerized systems and data-driven decision making claim to provide.

This chapter offers a guide to understanding and critiquing dominant smart city discourses through a discussion of key terms and concepts used in descriptions of smart technologies and environments. I unpack smart city justifications circulated by municipal and corporate executives and promises repeated by smart city developers and technology designers. While the chapter introduces some of the rhetoric and promises made by corporate smart city developers, I also highlight a range of counterarguments by those who regard these visions as neoliberal ideologies promoting inequitable or unjust technological and social practices. These critics envision a more human-centered conception of the city.

At present, the smart city concept and even the term itself are almost inseparable from corporate visions of what digital media, data, and urban space might be. This chapter is not meant to bolster or give credence to these perspectives. Instead, the reader should consider the promises and rhetoric described as offering only *one* perspective on how future cities might be built and governed, a perspective that is currently dominant but already being revised. The reader should critically consider what is being

At present, the smart city concept and even the term itself are almost inseparable from corporate visions of what digital media, data, and urban space might be.

left out or underrepresented in these urban imaginations, and the role of urban residents in cocreating urban places.

## What Are Smart Cities?

The day after the South Australian cabinet approved plans to continue Australia's first attempt at smart city development, a writer for the daily newspaper *The Advertiser* critiqued the term as a "glib phrase" that "carries all the conviction of a spin doctor's latest wheeze. It smacks of the politics of superficiality."[1] The author avoids a definition of the phrase, but ultimately expresses support for the project as an "exciting idea." This 1996 article resonates with popular press treatment of smart cities today. Articles covering smart cities rarely articulate clear understandings of what these cities are, but readily report on decisions made about smart city development or describe technologies to be implemented in these spaces. Robert G. Hollands, professor of urban sociology and oft-cited smart city critic, identifies similar rhetorical trends in scholarly and policy publications, noting that cities often congratulate themselves on being "smart" but rarely define the criteria by which to evaluate this claim or explain why being "smart" is so important.[2]

Definitions and characteristics of smart cities vary, and promotional materials make disparate claims about the value and purpose of these new constructions. Common to most of them, however, is a reliance on ICTs as the foundation and definitive quality of smart cities. Frequently, smart cities are regarded as urban environments where ICTs are aggressively implemented to collect data to support, monitor, and improve urban infrastructures such as transportation, waste management, energy consumption, and emergency response. ICTs are the substrates underlying the management of a multitude of networks; in a smart city they permeate nearly all aspects of everyday life to streamline urban activities and to gather and respond to system and client feedback in real time. At the heart of this understanding of smart cities is the ability to monitor urban activities and behaviors through pervasive, interconnected sensors, sentient objects, and high-speed Internet connections that translate urban activities into data. The desire to read urban interactions as data supports the idea of smart cities as data-based alert and response systems. Beyond being responsive to environmental and behavioral changes, smart cities are envisioned as predictive. Along with surveillance systems, "big data" analytics are touted as a means to predict trends or future urban activities and conditions.

Cities are already "smart" by several measures. Urban environments and populations repeatedly adapt to changing conditions, incorporate emerging technologies, and continually develop policies and social norms for managing complexity at macro and micro scales. Cities attract creative talent as knowledge economy hubs and innovation centers, which implies that the people who constitute the city are also highly intelligent. However, labeling a city as "smart" is a political and ideological choice. The term "smart city" implies a hierarchy in which certain cities are perceived as "smarter" than others and provides a general benchmark or goal for development; to attain this title, products and services can be sold and citizenry mobilized.

The term "smart" is strategically leveraged to advertise a city's logistical superiority. The ambiguity of the term enables organizations interested in various urban issues to utilize it to focus on different areas of innovation (e.g., in governance, public safety, transportation) or improvement (e.g., in health and well-being, sustainability, quality of life). Governing bodies such as the European Commission define smart cities as ones that use ICTs to create more efficient and engaging services for citizens and businesses, while the US Department of Transportation describes smart cities as urban forms that use technologies to aid mobility of people and goods; technology vendors note that smart cities implement digital tools that transform their core systems to optimize available resources and improve quality of life. Geographers Ola Söderström, Till Paasche, and Francisco Klauser conducted an in-depth analysis of IBM's Smarter Cities

The ambiguity of the term "smart city" enables organizations interested in various urban issues to utilize it to serve their own needs and to initiate different areas of innovation or improvement.

campaign and observed how the ambiguity of smart city concepts creates opportunities for corporations to intervene with their own definitions and scales for measuring "smartness." These authors argue that companies like IBM position technologies as more important than the outcomes or impacts of using these tools. IBM has specifically targeted cities and urban technologies as potentially lucrative markets, positioning its own products as "obligatory passage points" and the corporation as a necessary partner in smart city planning and development.[3] These findings imply that smart cities are more widely proposed than interrogated.

In practice, smart cities are defined as places where digital media are strategically integrated as infrastructure and software to collect, analyze, and share data to manage and inform decisions about urban environments and activities. As Antoine Picon, distinguished historian of architecture and technology, puts it, smart cities are imagined as sentient or "sensitized cities" that gain a heightened awareness of the world and of themselves through data and technology use.[4] Scholars from a variety of disciplines including urban planning and architecture, information studies, and geography have noted how blurring physical and virtual urban environments augments urban consciousness and produces more personalized or intimate relationships with urban space and place. Some of these relationships are sustained through smart city innovations like open data portals, sensor networks, and city government-commissioned mobile apps, but also through commercial locative and social media services, interactive public art projects, and digital street games. Still other engaging or intimate relationships with the city aren't observable or maintained through digital technologies at all and are often ignored in current models of smart or sensitized cities.

Planners, municipal officials, and members of the public have always been fascinated by idealized connections between technologies and cities and have been routinely aided by technologized means of governing and knowing urban space over time. Street lighting systems, transportation networks, telegraph lines, and high-modernist skyscrapers have all been celebrated as technologies for ordered cities that would usher in new eras of urbanism.

World's fairs and international expositions have regularly linked future cities with technological progress in their displays, in which modern technologies create rational and well-planned cities. For example, the popular General Motors Futurama exhibit at the 1939 New York World's Fair awed fairgoers with a city of tomorrow that assuaged traffic congestion through a network of automated highways. According to archived guest books and press coverage, World's Fair exhibits presenting films and models of automated cities and homes, high-tech transportation and communication systems, and innovative building materials tended to capture public and professional imaginations and offered images of comfort, control, and security. Depictions of these controlled cybernetic societies were common in science fiction films and television shows from the 1950s onward. Science fiction fascinations with control rooms or command centers as spaces that meld human and machine intelligence and celebrate constant surveillance and data flows for strategic decision making are reiterated in current smart city operations centers.[5]

Urban systems thinking from the 1960s imagined cities as series of complex, nonlinear, interactive systems in which urban activities could be thought of as information. *Urban Dynamics* by Jay Forrester, an engineer and computer scientist in the management school at MIT and innovator in applying systems thinking to urban spaces, was controversial upon its initial publication in 1969. Working with John Collins, former mayor of Boston, and Boston-based city managers and personnel, Forrester and colleagues proposed that computers could help analyze feedback loops between urban systems to model environments and behaviors. Models could be input into a computer to simulate and analyze specific variables that impact urban problems and development over time. Urban dynamics emphasized the idea that computational modeling could more accurately identify roots of urban problems within complex systems than could humans, who often identified and treated symptoms of urban issues rather than under-lying causes, leading to ineffective or even damaging urban policies.[6] Although systems thinking has been integrated into urban planning theories and approaches, in its early days it was widely criticized by scholars and government officials as an oversimplified way to analyze or evaluate social policies and urban activities.[7]

Smart cities can be understood through histories of urban imaginations that prioritize maintaining order and efficiency and fostering economic growth and competitiveness in global and regional markets through technological and scientific developments.[8] Globalization and labor mobility, rapid urbanization, and growing competition among cities to attract financial and human capital continue to pressure cities to do more with less. Within these contexts, optimization and sustainability emerge as reiterated goals that technological systems help attain by restructuring the city as programmed and programmable—constantly collecting, analyzing, and responding to real-time information. In terms of urban governance, smart cities can be considered as yet another proposed solution to the ongoing problems of administration and control within expanding and unpredictable urban environments.

"Smart cities" of the 2000s differentiate themselves from "intelligent cities" or "digital cities" of previous eras in their ability to respond to, adapt, and even predict users' needs and behaviors. In their survey of smart city definitions, professors of engineering and management Vito Albino, Umberto Berardi, and Rosa Maria Dangelico note that while "smart cities" once meant cities in which digital infrastructure and ICTs had been implemented, the term now implies that these ICTs are intended to optimize every urban system with the goal of enhancing services and residential life.[9] As Anthony Townsend, urban planner and internationally recognized smart cities consultant and author, summarizes, "Smart cities are places where information technology is wielded to address problems."[10] Current smart city developments are meant to address problems quickly based on huge amounts of data gathered through sensors and antennae that constantly monitor urban activities and environments. Industry press outlets, and urban and technology developers in the business of designing and implementing smart cities, note that these cities are defined by their ability, innovativeness, and agility in integrating intelligent IoT devices into urban development and planning.[11]

IBM, one of the technology companies leading smart city development in the early 2000s, uses "smart city" to describe how public services and infrastructures are "enhanced with information technology and data analysis."[12] Rio de Janeiro's Centro das Operações do Rio ("Operation Center" or OC) and Centro Integrado de Comando e Controle ("Integrated Center of Command and Control" or

Current smart city developments are meant to address problems quickly based on huge amounts of data gathered through sensors and antennae that constantly monitor urban activities and environments.

ICCC) are early, defining examples of IBM's smart city vision. Established in 2010, these big data centers created through a partnership between IBM and Rio's municipal government continuously gather and visualize data from approximately 30 public service agencies within Rio's city limits. The ICCC serves as the security and operations headquarters while the OC overlays information about several different service agencies including waste collection, transportation, and public safety with visualizations and alerts about traffic accidents, weather conditions, and power outages.

Sensors, cameras, and GPS installed on city streets and municipal vehicles collect and report real-time information to the data centers, where employees and software maintaining the feeds can identify patterns and locate issues or incidents to be ameliorated. When three adjacent buildings collapsed in downtown Rio in January 2012, public officials lauded the OC's almost immediate response. As the *New York Times* reported, OC employees directed ambulances and evacuators to the scene, shut down gas and power, and closed nearby subway stations, then tweeted warnings to avoid the area and had streets blocked to secure the vicinity.[13] The OC has been credited with improving Rio's disaster and emergency response systems and managing flood-related landslides. When Rio's mayor Eduardo Paes spoke at a high-profile TED conference in California nearly a month later, he video-conferenced with the multiscreened data center and uniformed employees to demonstrate the technological spectacle of monitoring urban activity and how he could govern his city from afar.

In 2011, before completing Rio's command-and-control centers, IBM trademarked the term "smarter cities," further solidifying a technology-biased perspective on the meaning and partnerships for building cities with the prefix "smart."[14] Leonidas Anthopoulos, business professor specializing in information systems, traced the evolution of the term "smart city" from 1990s usage of "digital city" and "virtual city."[15] "Digital cities" tended to describe online communities, widespread municipal Internet access, or digital portals displaying information about a particular city. A well-known example was Amsterdam Digital City (1994–2001), a virtual community enabling users to create homepages, newsgroups, and categorized areas of interest and chat spaces through an interface that resembled a city. Söderström, Paasche, and Klauser also trace the origins of the term "smart city" to the 1990s but notice that in mainstream English-language newspapers the term described cities that introduced ICTs or e-governance to automate municipal systems or foster economic development by attracting high-tech industry clusters.[16] Early examples of these 1990s smart cities include Multi-function Polis (MFP) in Adelaide, Australia, Putrajaya and Cyberjaya in Malaysia, and Tokyo's Teleport project, as well as 22 other Japanese cities slated to house approximately 400 "smart buildings."

From the idea of bringing the city or urban activities online, the term "smart city" developed in the 2000s to represent ICT integration into physical urban environments. However, the interconnectedness alluded to in these descriptions has been uneven. Edgar Pieterse, professor of urban policy and director of the African Center for Cities, has noted how the World Bank's influential City Development Strategy and related city development guides emphasize a connection between economic growth and sustainability and selective infrastructure investment. Drawing on Stephen Graham and Simon Marvin's foundational arguments about the privatization and "unbundling" or "splintering" of urban infrastructure, Pieterse notes that during the 2000s certain types of infrastructure development were seen as more valuable to economic development and urban management than others. Expressways, logistics ports, airports, and telecommunication networks that support economic growth, attract entrepreneurial talent and businesses, and improve the mobility and security needs of "high-end service and manufacturing sectors" were prioritized.[17] Smart city critics have argued that Graham and Marvin's "splintering urbanism" is reinscribed in smart cities as corporate-sponsored visions lead to social polarization and inequity through digital media implementation and data-driven analytics.

The selective investment in infrastructure and the types of activities and populations smart city developers recognize as valuable are central questions for subsequent chapters.

Much smart city critique has focused on ideologies shaped by industrial strategies and the development of centralized, proprietary, technology-centered urban administration and design. Prominent and repeated smart city characteristics are read as overly narrow in that they focus on technological infrastructures at the expense of social interactions and favor economic development, regional competitiveness, and efficient services above other urban development trajectories. As one of the initiators of these critiques, Hollands argued that dominant smart city models support current trends in entrepreneurial urban governance and the corporatization and privatization of public space.[18] Several scholars including Rob Kitchin, a professor and thought leader regarding relationships between urban spaces, software, and data, have positioned smart cities as emanating from (among other origins) a shift toward neoliberal entrepreneurship within city management that shaped later visions of globally competitive cities, sustainable cities, and urban theorist Richard Florida's idea of the creative city (or the prospect that culturally rich and socially tolerant cities attract talent and foster economic development).[19]

Perhaps the most extreme example of neoliberalism in smart city design and development is "smart-from-the-start" cities, new cities or districts built from scratch that adhere to some variation of smart city models (see chapter 2). These cities incorporate privately owned technologies and software on public streets and privatize aspects of public service provision and administration but are also built within free economic zones that subsidize transnational flows of enterprise and capital. Corporatization of urban management and neoliberal entrepreneurship are also evident in the private and public partnerships forged between technology industries, universities, and municipal governments in smart cities. Apart from municipal officials, none of these actors are democratically elected, they often function without public input or review, and they focus explicitly on investments and generating profit. This extreme privatization, deregulation of public-private exchanges, and the ways in which market economies and advanced capitalism have shaped smart cities led Adam Greenfield, urban designer, theorist, and prominent critic of smart cities, to argue that the smart city is "difficult to imagine outside of neoliberal political economy."[20]

Scholars and journalists have also critiqued the ways "smartness" is envisioned by corporations and city governments. Shannon Mattern, professor of media studies whose research focuses on urban space, architecture, and media infrastructures, lucidly summarizes a reiterated critique of dominant smart city imaginaries with her warning that "a city is not a computer."[21] This argument rests on the idea that the quantification and datafication of urban environments are shaped by and perpetuate a gross misunderstanding of what cities are and how they work. Smart city perspectives critiqued here prioritize the "smart" rather than the "city" in a manner that reenvisions all urban exchanges as measurable transactions to be read by computers and data analysts. Corporate or vendor-driven perspectives translate all urban issues into engineering problems that can be solved through quantitative methods and design thinking. Those who question dominant smart city models argue that top-down technological solutionism promoted by smart city developers evokes a myopic vision of the city as a place and a nearsighted understanding of digital media use within urban environments. In the following section, I highlight some of the ways these promises and critiques appear in justifications for smart city development.

## Why Build Smart Cities?

It is important to consider how smart city developers articulate the need for these urban forms. Critics of dominant smart city trends take issue with the entrepreneurial nature of their development. Meanwhile, smart city planners and enthusiastic CIOs reiterate explanations about why smart cities are needed now.

The key narrative framework used to describe the need for smart cities is that cities need to be updated to house the world's future population. Plans and presentations about smart cities repeat the statistic that approximately 70% of the world's population will be living in cities by 2050. However, cities are said to be broken or at least in need of a makeover. They are represented as polluted, congested, unsanitary, inefficient, dangerous, and uninformed (figure 1). Images of traffic congestion or of unwieldy crowds imply not just impending or actual overpopulation but abundance of entities and data points that need to be managed and ordered (figure 2).

The anticipated exponential rise in urban population and the space and resources needed to support it serves as an explanation of imminent realities and a situation that requires immediate action. To adapt and accommodate increasing populations and changing economic, environmental, and communication needs, cities must be flexible, efficient, and healthy in terms of living conditions and climate. While many smart city developers claim that cities are broken and need to be fixed, others present smart city development as a preventative measure. Urban transformation from disorganized organism to ordered,

**Figure 1**    Images of "urban problems" from New Songdo City promotional pamphlet. Source: Gale International and Kohn Petersen and Fox Associates PC.

streamlined, responsive layers of controlled technological systems becomes both the goal and the justification for smart city development.

While there are thematic overlaps among justifications made by smart city developers, technology companies, and public officials, each promise is self-serving.

**Figure 2** A vision of smart city "solutions" in Kansas City. Source: City of Kansas City, Missouri, http://kcmo.gov/smartcity/.

A company that specializes in energy-efficient devices constructs smart cities as solutions to environmental problems. Corporations selling high-tech lighting infrastructures emphasize public safety and security issues. If a smart city developer is able to provide network management services and broadband infrastructure, then the smart city as a responsive environment will dominate conversations. All of these claims consider smart technologies and initiatives as "solutions" that will "improve quality of life" for urban residents. As Siemens claims,

It's possible that in the future people will live healthier, more pleasant, and more relaxed lives in the major cities than they do today. But that will require cities to become smart. ... The path to that future does not lead back into a pre-industrial age. Instead, it leads forward to an age of digital technologies in which cities operate like large computers.[22]

Operating like a computer is presented as an urban ideal. Computers can retrieve, store, calculate, and process data. If the city is like a computer, it can be programmed to produce desired outcomes and structure urban interactions. As the following sections illustrate, benefits of computation are integrated into smart city narratives in ways that rely on emerging technologies and current visions of the future of computing such as artificial intelligence (AI), IoT, and big data. Therefore, critiques of smart cities and their promises often overlap with critiques voiced about these technology trends.[23]

Aside from the idea that computing power will save future cities, a few interrelated claims about smart city promises can be tracked. I've categorized these justifications as: efficiency, awareness and responsiveness, sustainability, economic development, and citizen engagement. The following sections examine how these claims are articulated in dominant smart city discourse.

# Efficient Service Delivery and Optimized Infrastructures

Urban planning and city management histories present a series of changing strategies for building more cost-effective, efficient cities in which urban resources are conveniently accessed. Geographers Shelton, Zook, and Wiig note the resemblance of smart city technoscientific efforts to past models of urban growth in times of austerity.[24] When global and national economies suffer, cities reorganize around new technology-oriented management strategies that restructure mobility patterns, service provision, and urban space. Transportation, waste and water, and communication systems are "optimized" through new technologies that produce more effective results at lower costs. In smart city paradigms, data "fuel[s] unhindered progress" and real-time responses to streamline inefficient infrastructures and save money.

Anchoring claims about the need for smart cities is the idea that acquiring more data about public service delivery and use will undoubtedly lead to more efficient city services. Service provision narratives typically involve stories about a city's shortened response times when dealing with power outages, rerouting snow plows to areas more heavily effected by winter storms, and reallocating energy resources to meet increased or decreased demand. Optimized service provision might also require just-in-time or on-demand services triggered by citizen requests. For example, public transportation services that mimic commercial, sharing-economy models have been incorporated into a variety of cities. Municipal apps or websites allow residents to request microbuses or carpool services when public transportation is not readily available.

In corporate smart city development, efficiency or optimization is prioritized as an end in itself and a means of maximizing economic growth, increasing revenue for local governments, and minimizing waste. Positioning efficiency at the center of urban governance ignores other values of urban life. The focus on efficiency and optimization of services through data collection influences the ways that the relationships between citizens and the city are perceived and framed. In smart city models that value efficiency and cost-effective services as primary outcomes, citizen engagement is often limited to customer service relations. Smart city critiques urge policymakers and technology designers to move beyond efficiency and optimization to think about other ways that cities and citizens can be smart or connected.

## Awareness and Responsiveness

Although the city is constructed as a chaotic place, companies like Cisco and IBM offer "solutions" to "urban challenges" and encourage improved "urban performance."

Urban problems are loosely categorized as public safety concerns (crime and emergency response), traffic congestion and restricted mobility of people and goods, job creation and economic growth, and inefficient resource and infrastructure management and service provision. The "solutions," which include linked data systems, ubiquitous cameras and sensors, and increased opportunities for data gathering, adhere to a customer service or concierge model of awareness and responsiveness. Smart city developers advocate for collecting and processing data to make more informed decisions and target municipal resources based on calculated need and demand. Scholarly definitions of the smart city reiterate this perspective. For example, public administration scholar Taewoo Nam and director of the Center for Technology and Governance Theresa Pardo describe smart city capacities this way:

> A smart city infuses information into its physical infrastructure to improve conveniences, facilitate mobility, add efficiencies, conserve energy, improve the quality of air and water, identify problems and fix them quickly, recover rapidly from disasters, collect data to make better decisions, deploy resources effectively, and share data to enable collaboration across entities and domains.[25]

This definition emphasizes awareness of urban problems through data accumulation and analysis and the ability of city entities to act on this information for the public good. As described above, awareness and responsiveness tend to be enacted through the surveillance of urban activities, transactions, and mobilities—seeing and knowing where objects and people are located in relationship to others, tracking how they move and consumption patterns. For example, Sensity Systems, which specializes in providing LED street lighting with Internet-connected sensors and cameras, emphasizes the language of surveillance as awareness in its promotional materials. The company's "solution" for cities, NetSense, highlights video surveillance and real-time data collection and transmission about parking and pedestrian activity as cost-effective ways to maintain safety and security on city streets. NetSense allows government employees access to this data to monitor energy use and respond to circuit outages within the city's lighting systems.

Surveillance and self-surveillance are not exclusive to the municipal scale but are expected to occur in the household and on the bodies of individuals as well. When I've asked representatives from smart technology companies how increased awareness will improve everyday quality of life, they recount a hypothetical story about a lost child. In this fictitious example, a young child gets lost on the way home from school. Luckily, the child is equipped with a tracking device that uses public Wi-Fi, sensors and cameras mounted on streetlights, or even drones to alert the child's parents and authorities of the child's whereabouts. In the end, the child is returned home thanks to the help of smart surveillance technologies.

Smart city promotional materials incorporate healthcare and geolocative wearable technologies into their justifications for the benefits of smart city life. Information from mobile phones can be accessed by city officials and health organizations to monitor the spread of infectious diseases or personal health by transmitting vital signs in real time.[26] Smart city devices like wall-mounted video conferencing between patients and doctors, or heat- and vibration-sensitive floor tiles that call emergency services, are noted as solutions for "aging in place." With IoT incorporated into the home, your medicine cabinet could remind you to take a pill or your refrigerator could warn you against eating too much ice cream and call your nutritionist when you fail to heed the warning. Other hypothetical scenarios rely on intersections of self-quantification and sustainability where residents receive alerts when they consume excessive amounts of water or electricity.

This surveillance-oriented perspective on awareness and responsiveness necessitates the datafication of urban activities or the transcoding of urban behaviors into data. Smart city technologies created to respond to problems or demands depend on computational capacity to read urban activities as quantitative data and then measure and visualize these activities. The desire to make all aspects of urban space and urban life visible and therefore knowable or actionable has prompted concerns over privacy, usefulness of data gathered, and the illegibility of certain aspects of urban life. How do smart cities account for urban interactions that cannot be observed or computed yet affect the progress and experience of cities? What are the ethics of surveillance and digital rights of citizens within the smart city? Can all of this data actually be processed in meaningful ways? And importantly, do these enhanced digital infrastructures and the data they collect actually lead to improved quality of life?

Although these questions tend to be asked more frequently, there is little leeway within current paradigms to account for them. Instead, quantitative measurements masquerade as objective, neutral indicators that tempt policymakers with clear, simplified representations of complex phenomena. Smart city governance and management models rely on the quantification and visualization of urban activities often without specific questions to guide the accumulation and analysis of data and without strategies for acting on what they find. Although technology designers and vendors selling software and hardware for collecting and analyzing big data offer scenarios in which accumulating a range of data streams might be useful, municipalities grapple with the issue of how to make these quantifications actionable in meaningful ways.

## Smart Growth and Sustainability

As one journalist claimed: "If today's cities were living things, they would be monsters, guilty of guzzling 75% of the world's natural resources consumed each year."[27] The smart city is the aspirational opposite. It is a blueprint or "greenprint" for how cities can accommodate increasing urbanization and population growth through the promotion of sustainable living.[28] Smart cities support a vision of the near future in which urban forms and management practices will prevent and remedy catastrophic environmental ills such as pollution, climate change, and competition for natural resources.

Smart growth and sustainability are major threads in narratives of how and why smart cities matter. For example, in Siemens's answer to the question "Why do we need smart cities?" the company responds with a list of answers.

> Because our energy reserves are limited. Because the importance of renewable energy is continuing to grow. Because we are being forced to budget our

use of resources. Because we have to realize that buildings and cities can play a far more significant role in this regard than we assume.[29]

Siemens's argument is that integrated technologies and data make cities greener, eco-friendlier, resource-efficient, and potentially carbon neutral. The company argues that integrating IoT into physical structures and management systems and reporting information about energy consumption to users in real time leads to cost and energy efficiency with universal benefits.

In urban planning literature, the smart city is read as an outgrowth of "new urbanism" or efforts to make dense, highly populated urban centers more "livable," "green," and sustainable environments. The connection comes from the idea that the "key to sustainability is information," that by collecting and analyzing data about ongoing interactions within urban environments, municipal organizations can make more informed decisions about how to regulate them.[30] By measuring elements like pollution, water and energy use, waste accumulation, and environmental factors like sun, wind, rain, and temperature change, smart city proponents aim to make cities more resourceful, ecological, and able to accommodate growth and change safely and cost-effectively. Data provides "intelligence" about systems and how layered systems interact. Sensors that measure variables such as $CO_2$ emissions and greenhouse gases or energy and utility use and report back to centralized or open-access websites and databases are common smart city initiatives.[31] The abundance of LEED-certified buildings, green spaces, public transport and biking infrastructures, and systems that recycle trash, water, and energy have led reporters and those branding these cities to regard them as "eco-cities."[32]

"Greenwashing" smart city initiatives and sustainability rhetoric are utilized to attract residents and businesses. Images of clean, green urban spaces counteract images of cities as polluted and unkempt. However, Valeria Saiu, researcher in civil, environmental, and architectural engineering, argues that smart city efforts and sustainability claims of zero carbon or "eco-city" status often fall short. Saiu outlines some major critiques of smart city design: that smart cities cater to elite clientele, employ overstylized and underthought technology or building designs, and lack citizen agency or investment in smart city concepts and development.[33] For example, residences in the Bo01 development in Malmö, Sweden were outfitted with large glass windows so affluent residents could enjoy water views even though these windows were not heat-efficient or cost-effective. Citizens aren't always engaged or invested in planning sustainable spaces and technologies and may be hesitant to utilize eco-friendly designs in ways or as frequently as intended. Furthermore, these ecological designs are not usually distributed evenly across all communities, which limits their effect.

**Economic Development and Job Growth in New Economies**

In December 2015, the US Department of Transportation launched a "Smart City Challenge." The challenge invited mid-sized cities to compete for $40 million to improve "transportation performance." The winning city needed to "demonstrate how advanced data and intelligent transportation systems technologies and applications can be used to reduce congestion, keep travelers safe, protect the environment, respond to climate change, connect underserved communities, and support economic vitality."[34] Nearly all applications noted how expanded transportation networks coupled with data about bus, bike, or ride share locations could save time and money and create new economic opportunities for residents through enhanced mobility. The Notice of Funding Opportunity for the Smart City Challenge drew an explicit connection between economic opportunity and data-driven environments:

> Cities with existing commitments to managing
> their data as a strategic asset and making open,
> machine-readable data available to the public ...

are also good candidates that have the necessary policy infrastructure to fuel entrepreneurship and innovation to improve citizens' lives, create jobs, and spur economic development.[35]

The Department of Transportation was not alone in its efforts to competitively incentivize plans for smart cities based on the promise of economic development. In 2012 the UK launched the Future Cities Demonstrator Competition which framed smart city benefits in terms of service delivery and new revenue streams from sales of technologies and services;[36] the Smart Cities Council Readiness Challenge Grant (2016) emphasized smart cities as a competitive advantage in the global economy.[37] Even funding initiatives framing smart cities in terms of green growth and sustainability link smart city models and technologies to enriched local economies.[38] Economic justifications for smart city development tend to revolve around three topics: increased savings for city governments, new revenue streams from the sale of smart city products and the incubation of businesses and talent, and attracting global businesses or new businesses, thus establishing the city as a hub for economic activity.

While the promise of lower costs is linked to the optimization of infrastructure and public services, the potential for revenues is embedded in the idea of smart cities as laboratories, petri dishes, or "test beds" for new digital technologies. Smart cities are promoted as incubators for digital entrepreneurship and markets for technologies and services thus developed. The promise of economic development often rests on the idea that a smart city will be equipped to research and develop, test, and then export cutting-edge technologies, management, or data services to other cities.

As valuable as developing technologies that can be exported and sold to other cities is the cachet of being able to do so. Smart city proponents emphasize the symbolic power of smart cities for economic development. The creation of smart cities is seen as an advantage in place branding and intercity competition. Municipal officials and CIOs welcome the idea that smart city development will cultivate an image of their cities as leaders in technology sectors and smart growth, and as innovative and invested in "upgrading" and improving the lives of their citizens.

Smart city development is promoted as a strategy for retaining workforce and startups as well as attracting new businesses and talent. Smart city master plans typically depict enhanced entrepreneurial relationships between city governments, business sectors, and universities in which all three entities work together to research and develop marketable technologies, cultivate high-tech businesses, and produce labor and talent to support economic progress. The smart city promises to support businesses in the new economy by providing high-speed networks, advanced business services, and environments where work gets done. Images from smart city master plans and architectural renderings emphasize these claims by including blueprints for corporate headquarters and multistory buildings that will house transnational business elites and their companies.

Additionally, ubiquitous connectivity and data-driven services are said to increase job opportunities for previously marginalized communities. Cities that aim to retrofit urban spaces with enhanced digital infrastructure adhere to ideas that expanded Internet access will alleviate digital divides and lead to increased job opportunities for local communities. For example, vision statements for the Smart City Challenge included discussions of how increased mobility through data-optimized transportation services and increased Internet access for residents would allow economically disadvantaged communities to connect to healthier food sources, social services, and potential employers more easily.

Although smart city developers tout promises of increased profit and presence within global economies, the economic benefits of smart technologies have been difficult to measure. While some cities report savings in terms of utility provision and use, smart cities have struggled to attract new businesses and residents. As will be discussed in subsequent chapters, the transnational headquarters expected to acquire space in smart-from-the-start cities have failed to arrive. Local universities and research facilities have moved in; however, businesses have been more hesitant to relocate or start up, and there seems to be no substantial movement toward increased economic development. At present, greenfield cities tend to cost more to build than the benefits they have shown in revenue or savings.

In retrofitted cities, the use of smart technologies for economic development is typically directed by local start-ups and entrepreneurs. Cities that have initiated smart city endeavors tend to tap public opinion regarding how newly acquired technologies and infrastructures could be used to accumulate capital. Local tech industry employees and entrepreneurs meet with city officials or join task forces to help shape directions for economic development.

## Civic Engagement and Participatory Government

The most elusive promise and justification for smart city development is civic engagement. Vendors and corporations advertise that smart cities provide new opportunities for "citizen engagement" but avoid defining what this engagement is or how it works. E-governance systems or websites that allow citizens to participate in town hall meetings from afar, lodge a complaint about housing violations from their living room, or email a public official are often used as examples of smart city civic engagement. Providing open datasets about 311 calls, area plans and census data, regulatory codes, traffic patterns, or budget information is also considered to be part of smart city efforts toward participatory government and engagement. These initiatives expand on ideas that efficient service provision and access to data about urban activities will increase civic engagement and efficacy. The connection between data provision and engagement is typically described through anecdotes about intrepid citizens who find inconsistencies in open datasets and report these deviations to authorities, or celebrated technology entrepreneurs who use city data to build apps.

Civic engagement is also understood as accessing convenient commercial services. At smart city conferences and conventions, speakers include high-tech stadiums or open-air malls in their plans for community and citizen participation. During the 2016 Gigabit City Conference, civic engagement was described as providing new ways to allow citizens to absorb content of interest to them (like watching the hometown baseball game) and providing more convenient public and commercial services. In this conceptualization, Wi-Fi installation in high-density areas promoted citizen engagement in the expectation that people would like to access information and connect to each other on the go.

Another perspective on citizen engagement comes from discussions of civic media and human-centered design. For example, Boston's civic innovation team New Urban Mechanics aims to develop digital technologies in order to improve city services. Unlike in other iterations of civic engagement, New Urban Mechanics representatives encourage a shift away from developing smart city technologies for cost reduction and efficiency, and embrace building trust between communities and cities as an alternate guiding principle. In this perspective, smart city technology and app developers consult communities and residents to discern their wants or needs related to city service provision.

Regardless of approach, citizen engagement technologies typically take the form of apps that allow residents to monitor and report problems and services. For example, many smart city apps function like web portals that aggregate municipal information, documents and forms, and government contacts. Other apps allow residents to photograph and report potholes or request public works maintenance, monitor school bus routes and schedules, or request resident input in the form of surveys or polls. Although collaboration between citizen and city is articulated in discussions of smart cities, the practice of collaboration is often limited within the technological affordances and imaginations of what citizen participation means in practice. The lack of meaningful citizen participation and engagement has led to critiques that the smart city doesn't address actual needs of urban residents and focuses on revenue streams or the convenience of tech-savvy elites rather than general citizen empowerment and social justice.

**Conclusion**

Each of these promises of smart city proponents is structured by the prevailing definition of smart cities as dependent on technological "solutions" to urban "problems." A city's success in meeting these promises is only beginning to be measured and held accountable. For example, the largest international professional association for technology-oriented research, the Institute for Electrical and Electronics Engineers (IEEE), has been working to develop standards for smart city performance based on International Organization for Standardization ISO 37120: "Sustainable cities and communities—Indicators for city services and quality of life," which describes a series of 100 indicators to measure city service performance and social conditions.[39] These standards, originally issued in 2014 and revised in 2018, put forth quantitative metrics for measuring categories such as economy, environment and climate change, governance, population and social conditions, safety, and water.[40] As will be discussed in chapter 3, these indicators have been adopted to delimit the types of data collected and analyzed in smart cities and are incorporated as framing devices within smart city dashboard systems for collecting and visualizing data.

Depending on which smart city definition is adhered to and which indicators are used to measure success, cities may fall within a wide range of outcomes. For example, professor of architecture Andrea Caragliu and colleagues note that the 1990s technology-centered definition of smart cities should be viewed as inadequate in today's urban environment. Instead they propose a definition of the smart city that focuses less on ICTs and more on investment in human and social capital to produce sustainable economic growth, management of natural resources, and participatory governance.[41] Current smart city development models often flip this emphasis to privilege technology as a means or determinant of economic development and resource management, neglecting important infrastructures for human and social capital, democratic processes, and equity in terms of per capita wealth, citizen agency, and access to resources and job opportunities.

As examined in the following chapters, each of these justifications for corporate or top-down models of smart city development has invited critiques from scholars, technology designers, urban planners, municipal officials, and community activists. As a starting point, people have questioned whether the smart city model is actually capable of delivering on its promises of improving urban experience and quality of life, and at what cost. Although smart city technologies and environments have recently proliferated, have we seen any evidence that enhanced digital infrastructure can benefit urban populations or significantly alleviate urban problems? What evidence are we looking for to measure smart city success and positive outcomes? Are there benefits for certain populations or sections of the city and not for others? What about significant urban problems that are left out of traditional smart city models such as failing school systems, poverty, neighborhood disinvestment, and lack of affordable housing? Reacting to the dominant smart cities concepts evaluated in this chapter, researchers and designers have suggested that cities look for more socially just and stimulating models for urban development and governance. The next chapter examines some prominent and emerging models of smart city development and the business practices and partnerships that make these urban projects possible.

# MODELS FOR SMART CITY DEVELOPMENT

In the previous chapter, I outlined justifications used to support particular conceptions of the smart city. This chapter focuses on these visions in practice. The following sections analyze three overarching models of smart city development: smart-from-the-start cities built from the ground up; retrofitted smart cities (preexisting cities outfitted with enhanced digital infrastructures, technologies, and city management services); and social cities where people use digital media to collaboratively address shared urban issues. Each model exhibits overlapping and distinct ideologies, plans, and policies behind its development. The politics of each model are highlighted and critiqued, and the conclusion presents an overview of funding sources, business plans, and partnerships employed to finance smart city development.

## "Smart from the Start" Cities

Smart-from-the-start cities are entire cities built from scratch with digital infrastructure and data analytics as integral aspects of their master plan. Although these cities are comparatively rare, press releases indicate that several greenfield cities are currently being planned in India and China, among other locations.[1] Other smart-from-the-start projects resemble business districts or sections of a larger city. The Gramercy District under construction near Washington's Dulles International Airport claims to be the first smart-from-the-start urban development in the United States,[2] and Alphabet's Sidewalk Labs is building a smart district in Toronto's waterfront that will house Google's Canadian headquarters among other businesses and residents.[3] Smart-from-the-start cities have been readily adopted in developing countries where there tend to be infrastructure gaps, burdened utility provision, and need for cost-effective methods of managing urban activities and monitoring pollution and traffic.[4] These carefully curated cities represent a determinist, leapfrog approach to urban development emphasizing a singular model of success for globalizing cities and focusing on technology and data as solutions to urban problems. As a result, these manufactured spaces have become emblematic of the promises and pitfalls of early smart city development.

Smart-from-the-start cities attempt to foster innovative business districts for profit generation, initiate urban and regional revitalization, and attract foreign direct investment and talent migration. Urban environments such as South Korea's U-cities, Hong Kong's Cyberport, Dubai's Media and Internet Cities, Kenya's Konza Techno City, Singapore's One-North, Tokyo's Ubiquitous Technology Project, Hyderabad's HITEC City, Dholera Smart City, and Mauritius's Ebene Cybercity (to name a few) are state-mandated or state-orchestrated nodes of global and local digital media and economic activity typically planned in partnership with transnational corporate entities. These enclaves coopt the title of "city" but share few social and political characteristics with preexisting cities. The products and services that render them "smart" are designed by recurring casts of corporations, which urban theorist Dan Hill refers to as the "Urban Intelligence Industrial Complex":[5] IBM, Cisco, General Electric, Siemens, Microsoft, Philips, Oracle, and other technology industry monoliths.

Smart-from-the-start cities differ in size and population and cost exorbitant sums to erect. Some are slated to be expansive, all-encompassing environments that house anywhere from 30,000 to 1,000,000 residents and cost billions of dollars to fabricate. Among cities currently under construction, PlanIT Valley in Portugal plans to house 225,000 people and cost approximately $19 billion,

Masdar City in the United Arab Emirates is designed for 50,000 people and estimated to cost $20 billion, while India's 100 smart cities are estimated to cost $1 trillion and house millions.[6] However, construction on many of these projects has been halted or delayed.

Though a subset of the full range of smart cities, these serve as models that influence wider smart city adoption. Companies involved in developing and planning smart-from-the-start cities indiscriminately export technologies and master plans developed for these environments to already existing cities across the globe. The Gale Corporation (Songdo's developers) and its partners (including Korean government officials and agencies) have been outspoken about their plans to internationally export the Songdo smart city model for profit. At a tech industry event in 2009, Stanley Gale enthusiastically announced his plans to build at least 20 similar cities across East and Southeast Asia.[7]

In particular, free economic zones sustain smart-from-the-start cities. These zones make smart-from-the-start cities feasible and render them attractive to developers and transnational corporations as spaces exempt from policies, taxes, and rules that apply to the rest of the nation-state. These sanctioned zones promote direct investment through tax subsidies and exemptions, cheap land rates and property taxes, and lax regulations on foreign direct investment. Keller Easterling, distinguished architect and urban theorist, describes "the zone" as "offering a 'clean slate,' and 'one stop' entry into the economy of a foreign country."[8] Easterling explains that zones market themselves as cosmopolitan spaces of "unencumbered wealth" free of traditional urban negotiations over issues such as labor, human rights, or inequality, and may cater to or sustain cultures and lifestyles inconsistent with the majority of national populations.[9] Nearly all South Korean U-cities are built within free economic zones; the best-known, Songdo, is situated squarely within the Incheon Free Economic Zone (IFEZ) that houses two other greenfield projects.[10] Masdar City resides in Masdar Free Zone providing 100% foreign ownership and exemption from personal and income taxes, with no import tariffs or repatriation of capital or profits.[11] Government spokespeople noted that most of India's 100 smart cities would be built within Special Economic Zones.[12]

Smart-from-the-start cities are more dependent on logics of capitalism and complex private and public partnerships than on any other aspects of development. These cities can be read as primarily economic endeavors that prioritize entrepreneurship over other urban values. Scholars situate smart city developments as new forms of "entrepreneurial urbanism" and neoliberal capitalism where the purpose of the city is to promote and foster economic growth.[13] The industry-sponsored advocacy group Smart Cities Council (partners include Cisco, GE, IBM, Mastercard,

Smart-from-the-start cities are more dependent on logics of capitalism and complex private and public partnerships than on any other aspects of development.

Microsoft, Verizon, Black and Veatch, Intel, Saudi Telecom, Siemens, Qualcomm, Neptune Technology Group, electric and metering technology companies, transportation and grid systems, and others) articulates the benefit of smart cities in primarily economic terms as well:

> The smart city movement is not just a trend—it's a race. It's a race to gain competitive advantage in the global economy. A race to attract jobs and talent.[14]

Here, attracting economic opportunities and repositioning cities as control-and-command centers within global economic networks are prioritized over justifications that emphasize resiliency, sustainability, and equity. Cities are framed as infrastructural management systems rather than places where people commune and live. The above quote asserts the imperative and the competitive urgency of building this type of smart city. From this perspective, the infrastructural smart city is necessary, and cities that adopt it first will be rewarded while others will be left behind.

Also left behind are disadvantaged or low-income populations. Municipalities and nation-states often pass special ordinances for private enterprises or state entities to acquire land at inexpensive rates or for states to expropriate land from existing residents (for example, Land Acquisition Ordinance 2015 in India or the series of land reclamation and compensation ordinances for IFEZ in South Korea). Land acquisition processes are driven by private investment and development plans, with government ministries or affiliates signing decades-long leases or selling land to private developers below market value. Ayona Datta, professor and prominent expert regarding smart city development in India, observes that, unlike in the United States or Western Europe, building smart cities in India and the Global South requires massive appropriation of indigenous land and agricultural or rural land.[15] Although there have been public outcry and lawsuits concerning land rights for smart city development, Datta notes that the Indian government didn't heed these calls, instead changing the Environmental Impact Assessment law to facilitate developers' claims and land use.

Slums and lower-income housing become dispensable structures that interfere with master plans, and ensuing gentrification limits affordable housing options. Several smart-from-the-start cities have displaced preexisting populations. In western India, the construction of the eco-city Lavasa reportedly evicted, harassed, or undercompensated residents of at least 20 villages in order to break ground.[16] Indian housing activists calculated that an average of six homes are razed and 30 people evicted per hour for smart city developments.[17] Once cities are built, new apartment, office space, and condo prices prevent original populations from returning.

Transnational corporations have been reticent or unhurried in locating their headquarters in smart-from-the-start cities. However, international and regional universities have been quick to take up residence or establish satellite branches.[18] Although Masdar City was designed to house 40,000–50,000 people, it has currently only a few hundred residents, most of them students attending the Masdar Institute of Science and Technology.[19]

Residents have only modestly relocated to fill the newly constructed office and apartment buildings. While new cities are always difficult to populate, the lack of residents in smart-from-the-start cities is particularly striking. ICTs and services designed for smart cities are intended to organize complexity, govern the mobility of goods and people, and manage limited resources more efficiently. When populations and urban activities have yet to take root, the city and the technologies meant to orchestrate it feel vacant or superficial. For example, visitors to smart-from-the-start cities often describe the cities as silent or empty.[20]

I've visited Songdo four times since 2009. On each visit I've had miles of sidewalk to myself and an open table at any restaurant in town (see figures 3 and 4). Office buildings weren't bustling and traffic seemed to pass through, possibly from the Incheon airport to Seoul. On pleasant days, Central Park was well used but never crowded, and streets lacked activity and signage of other metropolitan

**Figure 3**  An empty plaza in New Songdo. Photo by author.

areas. People I spoke with rarely thought of Songdo as a smart city, but merely a luxury residential area for Korean nationals. One interviewee, a university student who visits Songdo frequently because his sister and brother-in-law reside there, thought it was humorous and quaint that I talked about Songdo as a smart city. He had forgotten the city was branded as "smart" and never notices any innovative technologies. Several other interviewees echoed this perspective and agreed that they vaguely remember something about the city being "smart," but considered

**Figure 4**  Empty sidewalks and cafes in New Songdo. Photo by author.

this a sales gimmick to attract wealthy residents. They know the area as a luxury real estate development near the airport where wealthy Koreans live, and a place with a big park.

Part of the risk undertaken by developers is that their "city in a box" fails to attract creative talent and enterprise and never becomes a hub for urban innovation. In Sidewalk Labs' promotion of their Toronto district, the company recognized that top-down cities lack character and community and become less attractive to potential residents.[21] Executives for the project noted their eagerness to work with Toronto's communities to give the city a soul and figure out how digital technologies will be used.[22] However, Google's waterfront district has recently experienced a flood of experts on community engagement leaving the project due to disapproval over the unethical ways in which residents' data would be collected and shared.[23]

## Retrofitted Smart City

More frequently, already existing cities are outfitted with technologies and plans developed and tested in smart-from-the-start cities. The incorporation of digital infrastructure and data analysis to drive urban governance and management and respond to and influence urban activities is often referred to by industry and municipal executives as "retrofitting" a city.

As smart city concepts are embraced internationally, different regional or local models for retrofitting smart cities have emerged. Ari-Veikko Anttiroiko, a professor of local government management, describes Western efforts to develop smart cities as "disjointed," employing various economic models, public and/or private partnerships, and fragmented development plans and timelines within smaller geographic areas.[24] North American smart city initiatives differ from European and Asia-Pacific models in that they are more modest in their scope and budget and tend to rely on piecemeal implementation of corporate technologies. Initiatives from the United States, Canada, and South America focus on specific aspects of ICT implementation within a single category such as transportation, water and energy, or public safety rather than implementing digital technologies and data collection within all aspects of urban life.[25] Other researchers have noticed these differences too and critique the trend of awkwardly retrofitting existing cities with "smart technologies" that are not integrated or compatible with existing governance and social and spatial relationships.[26]

Companies invested in retrofitting cities with "intelligent" infrastructure note that although expensive, building smart-from-the-start cities is easier than outfitting existing cities. Interestingly, the barriers perceived by companies like Cisco, Microsoft, and IBM are qualities that define cities: people already live there, infrastructures are managed by different departments, and citizens have concerns about privacy, security, and equity.[27] In response to these perceived barriers, ICT corporations and smart city developers offer "simpler solutions" for interested cities. These products provide a la carte selections of small-scale or one-off projects such as installing networked parking meters or connected trash cans, sensors and digital lighting systems, or Wi-Fi-enabled public transit options.

Although the term "city in a box" is used as a critique of one-size-fits-all master plans sold by corporations, several corporations and consultants advertise "smart city in a box" packages, "comprehensive solutions," or "plug and play" services for smaller cities on a budget.[28] Companies that design and sell "smart cities in a box" embrace the potential replicability of their platforms in other cities, and the profit generated by that replicability. The extensive data analytics control-and-command centers implemented in Rio de Janeiro and New York by IBM have been packaged as a suite of software called the "Intelligent Operations Center" that can be bought as a whole or in parts to manage water, transportation, or public safety systems.[29] Versions of the Intelligent Operations Center have been sold to Singapore, Madrid, Beijing, Minneapolis, Dighi Port Industrial Area in India, and several other locations as part of their "city in a box" packages.

Nearly all ICT companies involved in smart city development offer some sort of "city in a box" package. In one example, Microsoft and Singapore-based Surbana Jurong partnered to sell a "smart city in a box" package to clients. Client cities chose from software and services hosted in Microsoft's cloud and presented through Surbana Jurong's dashboard apps to manage and monitor urban activities within categories of "sustainability," "efficiency," "people," and "security." The "solutions" that map onto these categories include energy and water management (sustainability); smart lighting, and data analytics for mobility and facility use (efficiency); fire and smoke detection and facial recognition (security); remote control air conditioning and lighting, and reporting apps (people).[30] Municipal officials mix and match these technologies and services, selecting from categories that fit their needs.

Although cities install "smart city applications," they may lack comprehensive development plans. Piecemeal technology implementation such as utilizing sensors to monitor waste or water provision follows recommendations by companies like Cisco and IBM that cities start with small projects showing "quick payback" to provide momentum for future initiatives. These small-scale projects become emblems municipal leaders use to perpetuate images of smart city development success and progress.

ICT industries and corporate partners influence smart city development in other fundamental ways. Cities interested in smart city development often begin their journey by creating "digital roadmaps" that align mayoral or municipal government digital priorities and strategies. By creating a roadmap, municipal executives follow best practices established by industry planning partners and advisory councils that recommend leveraging roadmaps to foster engagement from potential stakeholders.[31]

Retrofitted cities become test beds in slightly different ways than smart-from-the-start cities, serving as both

Retrofitted cities become test beds in slightly different ways than smart-from-the-start cities, serving as both showrooms and living laboratories for smart city roadmaps and technologies.

showrooms and living laboratories for smart city road-maps and technologies. Often called "living laboratories" by their developers, retrofitted cities create spaces where technologies can be integrated and tested within preexisting urban environments. The city in perpetual beta becomes a selling point for technology providers and private partners.

Rio, Santander, New York, and Singapore are only a few examples of cities utilized as showrooms for smart technologies implementation and marketing. Santander, a mid-sized city in northern Spain, has been celebrated as a premier example of an urban living laboratory and showroom. SmartSantander was funded by the European Commission (about 8.67 million euros) as a test bed for smart technologies and smart city development plans. In partnership with Telefónica, the University of Cantabria, and Santander City Council, the city installed 12,500 sensors measuring trash, parking, pedestrian and vehicular traffic, environment and climate, and energy and water consumption, among other variables. Data from these sensors are algorithmically assessed, and services are adjusted based on information received.

Santander also offers residents and tourists a smart-phone app, "The Pace of the City," a "participatory sensing application" that allows the city to push information and directions and enables users to employ their phones as sensing devices uploading GPS coordinates, sound, and temperature and advertising local events to the Smart-Santander platform. Scannable QR codes provide information about train and bus schedules or places of interest throughout the city, and an augmented reality app for Android and iPhone, SmartSantanderRA, was released to provide real-time information about 2,700 locations and access to traffic and bus schedules, beach cameras, and weather reports. Reports from SmartSantander note that due to these innovations, energy costs and trash pickups were reduced by over 20 percent, saving the city money and unnecessary labor.[32] Uses of technologies to inform citizens of available parking or municipal departments of water, light, or energy use in Santander have been lauded as success stories for how smart technologies can help to regulate and more efficiently allocate resources.

However, researchers evaluating smart city dashboards, data practices, and operation centers have noted how big data use to manage cities is not as seamless, comprehensive, or effective as sometimes claimed. In their ethnography of smart city systems in Rio de Janeiro, Christopher Gaffney, a geographer from the University of Zurich, and Cerianne Robertson, a research coordinator for a nongovernmental organization based in Rio, observed how hundreds of cameras and GPS devices installed throughout the city offered only a partial view of traffic conditions and security. According to researchers, closed-circuit traffic cameras were exclusively placed in wealthy neighborhoods and didn't provide a holistic account of urban mobility and congestion. The researchers identified other absences as the Operations Center did not monitor privatized train and highway systems. Rio's monitoring and alert systems have been said to noticeably improve traffic flows and shorten emergency response times in places where they are installed, which further exacerbates disparities and potential social polarization among urban communities.

Retrofitted cities typically employ surveillance technologies to become "smart." US cities including Los Angeles, San Diego, Miami, and New York have installed gunshot audio sensors attached to streetlights and rooftops such as ShotSpotter. These initiatives have been criticized by community members in neighborhoods where sensors are installed. San Diego residents complained that they were not part of the decision to install the sensors and that data collected subjects minority communities to overpolicing without building trust between officers and community members.[33] Technologies like ShotSpotter are read as Band-Aids or disincentives for police departments to spend time and money building trust and partnerships with community members. Gunshot sensor networks and other surveillance systems encourage officers to rely on automated alerts from a distance, bypassing social connections and outreach that could encourage citizens to contact officers when a crime or public safety incident occurs. Other critiques of police surveillance technologies revolve around their effectiveness; officers and police departments admit that although they respond to gunshot alerts more frequently, these responses do not necessarily result in arrests or solved cases.

In addition to public safety, surveillance networks have been implemented in retrofitted cities as forms of self-quantification or self-surveillance. In Surat, India, where rainy season flooding is a major concern, sensor and satellite technologies and automated weather stations combine data measuring temperature and climate with information about river and reservoir levels to activate early flood alert systems.[34] Barcelona and San Francisco have invested in municipal-owned or operated fiber optic networks, free public Wi-Fi, and sensors that monitor waste, air quality, and parking. Barcelona measures the success of its IoT network in terms of efficient resources such as water use in public parks, more reliable bus service, and city lights that generate profit by attracting people to active locations within the city.[35] In other instances, sensor networks are employed within electrical grids that utilize ICTs to detect, monitor, and respond to changes in energy or electricity use. Amsterdam is testing a system where homeowners install solar panels connected to smart grids and virtual power plants. The virtual power plant, an online platform called City-zen, collects information about household energy production and consumption and allows residents to store surplus energy on their home batteries or sell it back to the city.[36]

Chicago offers another example of retrofitting that integrates various networked technologies to improve urban awareness and response. The city has received praise from civic media technologists and smart city advocates for its "Array of Things" network. Array of Things is composed of 500 sensors installed throughout Chicago that collect real-time data about air quality, climate, noise, and traffic. The system was developed by University of Chicago researchers (in partnership with Argonne National Laboratory and the municipality), who describe the network as a "fitness tracker" for the city.[37] Like a fitness tracker, the sensors send data to apps and dashboards so users (such as city officials, software developers, and researchers) can monitor and influence traffic management or climate change through predictive analytics. Eventually, the data collected will be published to city-operated open data portals. Chicago's CIO hopes that communities will take ownership of the data and "figure out how to use it to address questions they have." However, there aren't many documented instances of this yet. Chicago has made substantial efforts to engage citizens in discussions and training about Array of Things and to address privacy concerns through events and outreach, but members of the public didn't participate in informing the project's initial conception or purpose.[38] Array of Things is slated to be replicated in cities such as Seattle, Denver, Mexico City, and Amsterdam, while cities in China, India, and Southeast Asia have also expressed interest.[39]

It's difficult to measure the success of retrofitted smart city initiatives when piecemeal "city in a box" offerings are installed. Many of these products and services aren't integrated with each other and output data into preestablished systems of governance and urban management. If employees aren't trained to respond to this data, are trained to respond in prescribed ways, or if resources aren't available to respond to data received, then promised smart city transformations won't happen. While organizations can sell smart technologies and offer visions for how these technologies should be used, cities must decide how and whether they can utilize the data provided in meaningful ways.

## Social Cities

Smart city planners and designers focus on technology use for seamless, "anytime, anywhere"[40] connection for managing urban space. However, the most successful smart cities, as deemed by corporate experts, awards committees, and industry advocacy groups, are not those that use technologies to ameliorate urban poverty, reevaluate discriminatory governance procedures and practices, or redistribute access to urban resources, but "those that can handle the speed at which technology grows" and embrace "disruptive" technologies to increase efficiency in cities through "live experimentation."[41] These spaces minimize or erase friction in favor of optimization and efficiency which tend to displace the social life of cities.

In opposition to this perspective, researchers and urban planners have suggested that smart cities start with sociality as an impetus for construction. Unlike vendor-driven, technological-determinist approaches, several smart city planners and researchers advocate for strategies that privilege the place of the city, experiences and social exchanges among citizens, and the placemaking activities they regularly engage in. Professors of architecture and urban design Katharine Willis and Alessandro Aurigi have suggested that smart city developers view the city as a series of ongoing, socially constructed activities that contextualize technology use within citizens' everyday lives.[42] Carlo Ratti, director of the MIT Senseable City Lab, and Anthony Townsend have argued that sociability rather than efficiency should be the "killer app" for all cities, including smart cities.[43] By focusing on efficiency, these authors suggest that smart city planners eschew foundations of civic society such as social cohesion and democratic governance in favor of optimization and environmental and behavioral control. Instead of employing predictive analytics that regulate urban behavior,

The most successful smart cities, as deemed by corporate experts, awards committees, and industry advocacy groups, are "those that can handle the speed at which technology grows" and embrace "disruptive" technologies to increase efficiency in cities through "live experimentation."

urban technologies could be built in consultation with citizens and could invite people to collaborate in shaping their urban environments.[44] In summary, a smart city should be a social city.

Social cities shift the smart city purview from collecting data about citizens to citizens as "produsers" of the city who are empowered through digital media use. Researchers Michiel de Lange and Martijn de Waal focus on relationships between digital media and urban culture and position the social city within conversations about participatory culture, collective intelligence, and do-it-yourself (DIY) hacker cultures and ethics where diverse populations come together to solve shared problems.[45] Adam Greenfield refers to a similar shift in power and design as a bottom-up "spontaneous order from below," or what Jane Jacobs referred to as an order produced through voluntary labor and activities of people on the street.

Unlike vendor-driven discourses about optimization and efficiency through technology use, a social approach to smart city development emphasizes creative uses of digital technologies in public spaces as practices of participatory culture. For example, Scott McQuire argued that large public screens typically used as digital billboards could be repurposed in ways that promote public interaction in city streets.[46] A culture and communication professor with an expertise in new media and urbanism, McQuire observed how the Public Space Broadcasting pilot project in

Manchester, UK fostered collective rituals and unexpected encounters between strangers by utilizing public screens to show community-produced videos, new media art, and interactive site-specific content programmed by various city councils and community organizations.

Artists and technology designers have utilized public screens and smartphones to encourage social interaction and playful exploration of urban spaces. However, these efforts are typically associated with creative placemaking initiatives rather than smart city efforts. For example, a local artist in Denver, Colorado, with funding from the National Endowment for the Arts and support from the Downtown Denver Partnership, transformed two city blocks into an open-air videogame arcade.[47] Residents used their bodies and mobile phones to control avatars (many of which depicted animated versions of local iconography and landmarks) and gameplay displayed on shared screens. The artist's intentions for the popular, monthlong public arcade echoed smart city initiative outcomes such as creating resilient cities, connecting people, and creating possibilities for new economic opportunities and safer streets.[48] However, the artist focused on street sociability, creativity, and play as a means toward these ends.

Emphasizing sociality and putting people first shifts smart cities discourse from being smart because of technologies to being smart because of people using and cocreating with these technologies within the places where they live. A recurring example of potential feedback loops between citizens, their everyday urban practices, and digital technologies is participatory open data initiatives. Several cities around the world maintain open data initiatives and portals where data about the city is freely accessible and can be used, downloaded, and modified by anyone with Internet access. Dataportals.org, a website maintained by data experts and representatives from government and nongovernmental organizations, has identified over 550 open data portals worldwide.

While some cities host myriad datasets and statistics about urban activities such as crime, energy performance, registered businesses, eviction notices, and food truck permits, many more host hackathons that train or encourage citizens to use this data for their own purposes. The participatory nature of the hackathon, which encourages citizens to engage with and recontextualize urban data in community-specific ways, also encourages the use of open data for citizen entrepreneurship.

Civic or open data hackathons have been used to bring stakeholders together to collaboratively solve problems specific to a certain location or community. For instance, Mayor Stephanie Miner of Syracuse, New York prioritized degraded infrastructure such as water pipes and city roads in need of widespread repair. In 2015, the city began soliciting help from regional technology startups and installing sensors known as SQUIDs (Street Quality Identification Devices) on city trucks and snowplows to monitor road conditions. Magnetic sensors were also installed on water mains to detect the location and magnitude of leaks. After accumulating water and road data, the city partnered with AT&T and Syracuse University to host two hackathons called the "Syracuse Roads Challenge" where attendees were encouraged to utilize city data about transportation infrastructure to generate new ideas for improving mobility and road conditions. The mayor and chief data officer describe the ideal effects of hackathons as extending beyond creating apps or new products for infrastructure improvement, toward an investment in collaborating with community members to understand their city. As Syracuse's chief data officer explained, "When the city makes data available to the public, people can see how the city works. ... When people see where snow plows go, they can help us work better, continue our conversations across platforms, and enable us to come together to tackle this challenge."[49] In combination, data collection, open data, and hackathons are often conceived of as ways to start dialogues and foster collaborations between citizens, researchers, corporations, and municipal government about shared and significant urban issues.

The social cities concept doesn't critique the idea that digital media can be beneficial for urban citizens and governments but critiques the ways in which digital media within cities have been envisioned and embraced. Social cities discourse remains focused on digital media infrastructures and data within urban environments but proposes more participatory, open, or bottom-up alternatives for interaction. Social city advocates urge different ways of creating and implementing digital technologies, methods for collecting and utilizing data, and end goals for urban experience and development.

Emerging social city paradigms emphasize citizen engagement, stewardship, and active production of the city by citizens within democratic or grassroots structures, rather than citizens as bystanders that produce data for a black box. Saskia Sassen, an esteemed urban sociologist and authority on processes of globalization and human migration, has incorporated these perspectives on citizen-driven smart cities in her call for "open-source urbanism," where a city and its citizens leverage personal urban experiences to talk back to powerful actors attempting to transform urban space.[50] She envisions utilizing ICTs in a kind of "urban Wikileaks" in which systems are created to harness citizen perspectives and redirect flows of urban knowledge and information from neighborhoods to municipal departments, and horizontally so that citizens can engage with and learn from each other.

Some technology designers have taken this vision to heart in their design of smart city technologies. For example, LocalData, an app launched by three Code for America fellows in collaboration with the City of Detroit, collects and maps community-generated data about neighborhood conditions such as building and property damage, delivery routes for goods and services, vacancies and abandoned buildings, and environmental issues.[51] The noncommercial app puts professional planning tools in the hands of community members and neighborhood organizations to facilitate urban planning efforts among citizens. Similarly, community members worldwide have utilized Kenya-based software platform Ushahidi to collect and visualize crowdsourced and geo-coded information in real time, informing fellow citizens during emergency and recovery situations and protests or elections. Since its availability in 2008, Ushahidi's crowdmapping software has been regarded as more effective and efficient than centralized government efforts at responding to and gathering information about environmental and political crises or sexual harassment and corruption. The Ushahidi platform has also been utilized by urban community organizers to map bike routes and cycling incidents, generate community-sourced travel guides, or locate Christmas light displays in a particular city.

The social city model, more than smart-from-the-start or retrofitted city models, highlights the fact that most people have some access to mobile or digital technologies on a daily basis and knowledge or opinions about how to fix shared urban issues. Citizens utilize digital media to demand access to resources that meet local needs and experiences of urban place and potentially to reevaluate discriminatory governance procedures and practices. The concepts behind social cities are related to emerging ideas about smart citizens and citizen engagement elaborated in chapter 4.


## Business and Funding Models

### Vendor-Driven Echo Chambers

Smart city development has been significantly shaped by corporate markets and technology companies. Vendors that sell "smart technologies" drive design and propagate needs for the products and services they sell. These actors play three roles: they create or consult on city master plans, establish private-sector partnerships with municipal governments, and sponsor and advise organizations that create best practices and awards for smart city initiatives. Cities awarded a challenge grant might receive consultations, workshops, and even services from technology companies associated with the grant. For example, a Smart Cities Council Readiness Challenge Grant offered winning cities "a free citywide network, a street lighting audit, a buildings audit and much more," including "hundreds of thousands of dollars in help, products and services" provided by the same corporations who sponsored and evaluated the award.[52]

By participating in these competitions, municipal governments are uniquely exposed to corporate smart city development models. Cisco provides one example of this smart city matrix. The corporation partners with smart city development and advisory councils and offers funding to potential smart cities through its City Infrastructure Financing Acceleration Program.[53] The company prepared ICT master plans for at least four smart cities in India and collaborated with the Electronic City Industrial Association (ELCIA) to establish a hub for IoT and software development.[54] Cisco also advises, partners with, or provides technology or infrastructure management services to nearly all cities mentioned in this book, including Songdo, Kansas City, Chicago, Barcelona, and many others. Further illustrating this echo chamber is Marketplace.city, the 2017 World Smart City Expo Innovative Idea Award winner. The site connects governments with private-sector companies looking to sell smart city "solutions." The project itself reinforces current development models in which cities literally buy into technology company designs as clients. This database and matchmaking service positions vendors as visionaries and drivers of smart city development and was deemed uniquely innovative by an organization sponsored by technology companies.

Smart city development ecosystems reify ideas and definitions about what smart cities are, who they're for, and how they're built and financed. Narratives that idealize smart cities as exemplary urban forms originate from outside municipalities and tend to be articulated by actors from private technology sectors. These organizations have internal labs or initiatives dedicated to smart city development. IBM established the Smarter Planet initiative in the early 2000s, Cisco maintains Smart + Connected Communities initiatives, and Microsoft works on smart-city-related projects under its CityNext program. Mastercard rebranded its payment products and services and partnered with public- and private-sector entities to offer "connected solutions" as part of its City Possible initiative.

These companies consult cities, serve on advisory boards, or sponsor organizations that advocate and advise smart city development: Smart Cities Council, Digi.City, Smart City World Expo, Gigabit Cities, etc. These organizations issue reports and guidelines on smart city development, and offer awards and funding opportunities to cities. The Smart Cities Council publishes a free "Smart Cities Readiness Guide" offering checklists to determine your city's smart development status. Each chapter presents pages resembling advertisements for ICT company services and products for sale. Checklists include categories such as instrumentation, connectivity, security and privacy, and data management, and then suggest technologies that meet category targets. Organizations like Digi.City claim to offer best practices for smart city officials; a related organization, Smart Cities Connect, states that "we accelerate the growth and empowerment of smart cities" through webinars, coverage of best practices, trends, case studies, and conferences. The organization also hosts "an exclusive city-first peer network" where professionals and elected leaders can share information about smart city development.

Representatives from these organizations speak at international conferences such as IEEE, think-tank-hosted symposia, and smart city summits and expos where city officials and academics are also present. Rarely are there any dissenting voices at these conferences. Instead, conferences bolster smart city development planning and partnership echo chambers, with policymakers hearing reinforcing voices and perspectives. Smart city expos and events offer opportunities for municipal executives to interface with startups and ICT companies selling products and services. Blurring boundaries between public and private sectors, summits and conferences such as Smart City Expo fill exhibitor halls with municipal representatives and ICT companies demonstrating hardware, software, and master plans they've adopted as well as a space where startups can pitch services and products to potential investors. These events sometimes offer "matchmaking sessions" where technology companies are paired with cities to discuss products and services.

## Funding

A 2014 survey of US-based municipal executives conducted by Cisco and Smart Cities Council indicated that acquiring and maintaining funding was the biggest obstacle for smart city development.[55] (This Cisco and Smart City Council report is an example of the corporate echo chamber mentioned in the previous section. Cisco found that funding was an obstacle to smart city adoption, published a narrative about their findings, and then developed the City Infrastructure Financing Acceleration Program in order to fund cities purchasing Cisco products and services.) The cities surveyed currently use or planned to acquire funding from government-issued bonds, user fees, public-private partnerships (PPPs), or finance opportunities. Smart-from-the-start cities generally utilize multiple financing strategies including PPPs, equity investments, and debt markets to finance their projects. Depending on federal or state policies, PPPs for smart-from-the-start cities include national and international partners. For example, several Indian smart cities are funded from PPPs with Japan International Corporation Agency, UK, France, and Singapore global consultancy firms, IBM, Cisco, Microsoft, US-India Business Council, and a range of local and state agencies.[56] To complete construction of South

Korean U-cities, national government agencies (Ministry of Information and Communication and Ministry of Construction and Transportation), municipal governments, domestic IT and construction chaebols (LG, KT, Samsung, and POSCO Steel), international developers (Gale Corporation), IT corporations (Cisco, 3M, United Technologies), international architects (US-based Kohn Pedersen and Fox), domain experts at Korean and international universities, and high-tech consultants came together as sponsors and collaborators.

Competitions and grants have proliferated that promise funding from federal governments, private foundations, or corporate sponsorship in the form of financial awards, products, or services. Indian smart-from-the-start and retrofitted cities were selected through a government-organized "City Challenge Competition"; the US Department of Transportation and Infrastructure Canada held highly publicized Smart Cities Challenges. Across Europe, several cities have received generous funding from the European Commission's 7th Framework Program for Research and Technological Development (FP7 grants) to develop smart city projects. The program, lasting for seven years (2007–2013), awarded 50 billion euros to projects that strengthened European scientific and technological industry, funded research that supported EU policies, and encouraged international competitiveness for EU member states. FP7 grants directly financed smart city infrastructure and technology development, provided funding to researchers, and in some cases subsidized and incentivized resident participation in smart city initiatives. As part of Amsterdam Smart City, partially supported by FP7 funding, homeowners and housing developers applied for up to 2.6 million euros to retrofit buildings with technologies that would significantly reduce $CO_2$ emissions and connect to smart grids.[57]

Industry-sponsored US Ignite, Smart Cities Connect, IDC, and Smart Cities Council fund a variety of grants and awards including Smart City Readiness Challenge Grants, Smart 50 Awards, and the IDC Smart Cities North America Awards. International cities compete for World Smart City awards at Smart City Expo, and IBM holds its own Smarter Cities Challenge. Organizations such as Bloomberg Foundation, Code for America, Knight Foundation, European Innovation Partnership on Smart Cities and Communities, and Digi.City all offer funding for smart cities initiatives.

**Public-Private Partnerships**
Smart city advocacy organizations also promote the public-private partnerships that fund smart cities. These industry-sponsored advocacy organizations serve as liaisons or connectors between corporate entities and municipal governments willing to invest in smart city efforts. Smart-from-the-start and retrofitted cities are commonly

constructed through PPPs, or contractual agreements between federal, state, or local agencies (public sector) and for-profit organizations or corporations (private sector). Under these agreements, private-sector partners tend to take on more risk and management responsibilities and are compensated in terms of sales, service provision, and/or performance. These are typically long-term or multi-year partnerships.

In smart city development, there tend to be three overarching business models in terms of PPP agreements and project management: build-operate-transfer (BOT) (sometimes build-own-operate-transfer), build-operate-comply (BOC), and municipal-owned deployment (MOD).[58] A city may choose to be the sole investor, as is the case with a build-own-operate (BOO) model, and maintain more control over financing, return on investment, and smart city network operations, but this financing model is relatively rare in comparison to PPPs. The build-operate-transfer model (BOT) is fairly common and exemplifies the exponential risk and investment taken on by private-sector partners. In this model, private-sector partners install, deploy, and manage infrastructure and services for a prescribed period before management responsibilities are transferred back to the city. A municipality may choose to employ an open business model where the city establishes guides and regulations for right-of-way and contracts various companies to build infrastructure and provide services.

While PPPs and BOT are popular financing strategies currently, researchers and analysts from private and public sectors note that PPPs for infrastructure projects tend to fail or collapse. In addition, market borrowing and debt financing of infrastructure carry substantial amounts of risk and uncertainty.[59]

While the trend of receiving outside expertise continues, so do efforts to cultivate local talent in data analytics, coding, and smart city development and governance. Encouraging citizen entrepreneurs, funding for local start-ups, and local university professors and graduate students to develop technology and/or analyze data are forms of official or unofficial smart city initiative partnerships.

## Conclusion

Chapter 1 introduced some smart city justifications and promises that are currently circulating. Chapter 2 has focused on dominant and emerging models for instituting smart city plans. While smart-from-the-start and retrofitted cities represent what some scholars refer to as Smart City 1.0,[60] the social city proposes an alternate idea of technology use to foster democratic processes, citizen efficacy, and collaboration.

Reports and white papers issued by companies like Smart Cities Council and smart cities divisions of Cisco and IBM present best practices that place the companies themselves as instrumental drivers and necessary partners toward smart city "readiness" and development. These documents, conferences, funding opportunities, contests, and awards play dual roles in smart city development: they report findings and convince potential adopters simultaneously. By selling a particular smart cities paradigm, they are selling their own products and services.

Too often, private-sector partners maintain disproportionate influence and benefit from smart city development. Critiques of smart cities as undefined, lacking prescribed purpose, assessment, or recognizable widespread benefits open up more space for private enterprise to dominate. If the same companies that sell smart technologies shape understandings of urban problems and initiatives proposed to solve these problems, then municipalities are subject to one-size-fits-all corporate smart city models. Some public-sector resources such as the National Institute of Standards and Technology and a US Department of Commerce framework for smart city development are under way in the United States.[61] However, federal resources for smart city development rarely question or critique underlying smart city concepts or goals. At best, national programs create guides and best practices for creating roadmaps, open data plans, and funding opportunities for interested city leaders.

The next chapter focuses on technologies and assumptions about technology use that inform smart city perspectives. While several "smart" technologies have already been mentioned, the chapter summarizes technology designs that are commonly sold within smart city circuits and unpacks the stories told about how these technologies ought to structure urban space and urban life.

# SMART CITY TECHNOLOGIES

Dominant smart city conceptualizations position digital innovation and ICTs as central to urban development and administration. "Smartness" is framed as generated by technologies installed and implemented, and to some extent by how they're used and by whom. Smart city exceptionalism is understood through the simple assertion that if cities incorporate ICTs and data analytics, their performance will be improved. Through contemporary computing trends such as big data, cloud computing, and IoT, smart city master plans integrate information about urban activities to present cities as holistic, pervasive computing systems where all observable interactions and exchanges are monitored and connected.

This chapter introduces several technologies and platforms currently in use or under development for optimizing infrastructure and gathering and analyzing data about urban activities and systems. Technologies already implemented in some cities—gigabit networks, parking apps, streetlight and traffic sensors, open data platforms, automatic climate control, and water recycling systems—are a few examples of technologies proposed for smart cities. This chapter provides an overview of how these technologies are imagined to contribute to smart city management while introducing some debates and controversies around their implementation.

**Smart City Technologies**

As discussed in chapter 1, digital technologies are framed as essential catalysts of urban transformation within smart cities discourse. Smart cities as urban strategies for improving all aspects of everyday life and municipal service provision are celebrated as "strictly technology-sponsored empowerment" for urban residents.[1] Justifications for smart cities (efficiency, awareness and responsiveness, security, sustainability, economic development, and civic engagement) rely on technologies to function. In particular, planners and researchers focus on integrating big data, IoT, cloud and IT infrastructures, and mobile and social media as key components of smart city technological development.

In a 2016 report, *Trends in Smart City Development*, the National League of Cities envisioned how smart cities will integrate digital technologies into everyday life. In this imagined, not-so-distant future, a person wakes up in a house filled with artificial intelligence systems that automatically personalize room temperature and light levels, begin to monitor personal vital signs, and archive health data. Outside, city streets filled with autonomous vehicles and ride-sharing systems have made traffic, traffic signals, and parking garages obsolete. Digital kiosks resembling LinkNYC's transformed phone booths alleviate digital divides, while facial recognition software and gunshot detectors linked to police databases keep citizens safe. The environment is cleaner, the city is safer, and people are happier due to ubiquitous, networked ICTs.

Smart city research and development labs at Microsoft, IBM, Siemens, and Cisco promote these products, services, and the relationships they produce as urban ideals. For example, Microsoft CityNext promises that the adoption of "world-class technology" will "empower cities to be more sustainable, prosperous, and inclusive."[2] Similar language and offerings are repeated on other company websites targeting municipal officials, promising to "infuse intelligence" into their civic systems to improve citizens' lives. These technologies are affixed to homes and office buildings, lampposts and trash cans, and to fixed assumptions about urban space and human-computer interaction. Rather than being integrated into urban environments and behaviors, technologies are stamped on the city, and on all cities in the same way. While technologies may be state-of-the-art, they can't adapt to diverse urban conditions or emerging ways in which people make technologies meaningful within everyday urban contexts. Tensions exist within technology vendors' stories about smart cities, the types of technologies produced for cities, and who maintains control over how these technologies are implemented and used.

During the early 2000s, Mark Weiser's research on smart homes and offices, developed while chief technology officer at Xerox PARC, was often evoked by smart technology designers and academics to explain pervasive computing opportunities, sensors, and networks then being designed for urban spaces. The prevalence of computing opportunities ingrained "in the woodwork, everywhere" stems from Weiser's vision of what computing in public and domestic spaces might become.[3] According to him, computers would be embedded in the "most trivial things" of everyday life such as "clothes labels (to track washing), coffee cups (to alert cleaning staff to moldy cups), light switches (to save energy if no one is in the room), and pencils (to digitize everything we draw)." We would dwell with computers rather than merely interact with them.[4] However, as computer scientist Paul Dourish and anthropologist Genevieve Bell observe, ubiquitous computing paradigms employed in smart cities of South Korea and Singapore (for example) deviate from Weiser's vision in technological form and use. In these cities, ubiquitous computing and smart technologies are envisioned not as a "third wave in computing" but a utopian end state fueled by commercial, large-scale infrastructures that enhance corporate efficiencies.[5]

The technological vision for smart cities stems from an embrace of new media as the revolutionary future present, one that replaces local culture with digital culture. Simplifying and streamlining complex relationships attracts municipalities, as does revolutionary rhetoric about how the world will change for the better with digital intelligence. In conversations with constituents, cabinet members, and media outlets, municipal officials repeat promises of utopian smart cities that govern responsibly, respond to immediate needs, and prevent issues before they start.

Although smart city software and services are yet to be wholly implemented, three general schools of thought emerge in regard to ICT implementation. One perspective, supported by corporate vendors and celebrated by smart city consulting firms, is the blanket approach. From this perspective, the city should be covered with sensors and monitoring systems. Every object and person will eventually be linked to networked information systems, and everything and everyone will generate data. Expansive public and private Internet infrastructures become essential substrates supporting this vision, which is why many

The technological vision for smart cities stems from an embrace of new media as the revolutionary future present, one that replaces local culture with digital culture.

smart city developments begin with national or municipal mandates to construct comprehensive or high-speed information infrastructure.

Another approach to smart city technology implementation is more moderate and intentional in that technologies are designed and deployed to meet specific goals. One smart city initiative, Smart City Wien in Vienna, Austria, is an example of this second perspective and is said to have developed from local IT industry's call for municipal recognition and support. Smart City Wien strategies and objectives position "productive use of innovations/new technology" in the service of "radical protection of resources" and a "socially fair quality of life." In contrast to other roadmaps and development plans, Smart City Wien specifically describes and evaluates the resources to be protected and the characteristics of high quality of life, prioritizing specific outcomes achieved through ICT innovation and adoption. For instance, Vienna's smart city development objectives are primarily concerned with environmental sustainability and climate change. The first set of objectives aim to reduce carbon emissions and energy consumption while increasing renewable energy sources in public and private spaces that exceed European Union climate protection targets.[6] The primacy of environmental and sustainability concerns and leveraging ICT and transportation networks to achieve efficient resource allocation reverberate throughout the projects slated for the city. Additionally, the city aims to implement technologies or design nontechnological ways to ascribe citizens active roles in "controlling additional areas of daily life."

A third perspective pushes Smart City Wien's approach to citizen control even further. A people-led approach to smart city technologies is often mentioned by municipal officials and smart city planners as desirable but difficult to accomplish. This approach focuses on collaborating between various urban communities, integrating citizen input into smart city technologies and network design, and/or giving citizens control over how technologies are utilized in their communities. One example of this approach is Community PlanIT, an online gaming platform developed by the Engagement Lab at Emerson College that brings citizens and municipal organizations together to foster deliberation and discussion in city planning processes. The platform was used to create Detroit 24/7, a digital game initiating and supporting discussions regarding long-term urban planning for Detroit. Over 1,000 people participated in the project, and their thousands of comments and ideas were incorporated into the city's Strategic Framework Plan. All comments were compiled and visualized as open, anonymized datasets available online to Detroit residents and organizations.

The following sections describe some of the hardware and software that connect to and compose smart city networks, and the outcomes these technologies are expected to achieve. Ultimately, the chapter identifies two different understandings of smart city technologies: the promise of an "enhanced urban experience" versus cautionary tales based on how these technologies are currently employed. This chapter also highlights how the same technologies and digital activities (sensors, public Wi-Fi, big data, smartphone apps, and IoT) have been implemented in some cities as efforts toward efficiency and optimization and in others as tools for equitable access to public services, creating sustainable environments, and encouraging community engagement.

## Open Data and Real-Time Data

While smart cities adopt new technologies, they also utilize preexisting technologies and data in more "open" or public-facing ways. A common practice among municipalities is to create user-friendly, e-governance portals that aggregate city services and information in digital formats: contact information for government representatives and offices, local news and events, links to forms or license applications, or online payment systems for fines and tickets.

Another version of smart city portals incorporates links to open datasets that can be viewed and downloaded by members of the public. Among other organizations invested in smart cities and city management, the World Bank offers toolkits for public-sector managers about benefits, procedures, and best practices in establishing open data initiatives.[7] Hosting open data is seen as advantageous for fostering innovation and collaboration among individuals and between individuals and government or nonprofit sectors. The toolkit lists some benefits of offering datasets about cities to anyone with Internet access: government transparency, potential public service improvement, social innovation and economic growth, and efficiency in interdepartmental communication and information sharing.

There are a variety of open source and vendor services for hosting open data catalogs offering different functionality to managers and users. The City of Los Angeles, which utilizes the cloud-based commercial platforms Socrata and ArcGIS, supports a suite of data manipulation and visualization tools as well as extensive open data catalogs including geospatial information. In addition to creating maps and visualizations of data collected from the catalog, users are able to share their maps and visualizations through the website. The city reports that over 40 public apps have been created and released based on open geospatial data. One app garnering attention in LA, a city dependent on driving and highway use, is StreetWize, which maps construction projects and roadwork throughout Los Angeles. Another open data project, Vision Zero, visualizes annual pedestrian and vehicle fatalities and severe injuries since 2015. Two other street- and transportation-focused apps map street cleanliness (CleanStat) and provide a story map of all roadwork completed since Mayor Garcetti took office in 2013 (Road to 2400).

A unique example of data sharing from London is a platform called OpenActive that is aimed at promoting health and well-being rather than government transparency and improved public services. The platform creates a space where sports and physical activity providers citywide can share information about their facilities, events, sports matches, and exercise schedules to facilitate physical activity with others. In addition, residents can locate exercise partners or trainers, gyms or playgrounds, pickup games or races, or join group bicycle rides or runs.

Real-time data provision is also employed as a strategy to improve service efficiency and coordinate urban activities. Utility service providers, municipal institutions, and government agencies have utilized popular social media sites such as Twitter to relay real-time information to citizens and residents. Smart city apps utilize affordances such as geolocation and mobility to provide information about transportation routes and schedules, nearby events, advertisements for retail stores or restaurants, or public safety and municipal contact information. Apps and smartphones have also been employed as tools for reporting information about urban activities and accessing information in transit. Combinations of services and hardware that many citizens already use, like smartphones and social media, are being utilized more deliberately by smart city developers as tools for data collection. Building inspectors in Mobile, Alabama have used Instagram to document and report building code violations and abandoned buildings.[8] As part of its smart city efforts, the city of Stockholm, Sweden has created several apps for citizens to report information to municipal departments. The "Make a Suggestion" app allows citizens to report street lamps that are out of order, roads that need repair, graffiti, or overflowing trash bins. In Boston, the New Urban Mechanics team created a similar app that allows residents to upload photos of potholes and request services from the city. Boston is also one of several cities (including New York and Rio de Janeiro) to partner with Waze, a popular crowdsourcing traffic and navigation app, to update real-time data streams about traffic patterns and congestion.[9]

Other smart apps expand real-time information access to the home as well as the city street. The Living PlanIT app and portal for PlanIT Valley in Portugal allow residents to access real-time information about city services and transportation schedules, request services, as well as monitor and respond to changing conditions in their home such as climate control or lighting systems while on the go. Stockholm's "Absence app" allows parents to report to public schools when their child is out sick, and the city of Oulu, Finland has created several mobile apps that manage daycare employees and children's absences in real time. The use of mobile phones connected to social media and data services, cameras, home Internet connections, and centralized city data centers is emblematic of the types of real-time, big data collection that fuel smart city services. However, these public-private services that depend on geolocation and networked data flows between urban residents, private service providers, and government entities are critiqued for placing access to information above citizen engagement or privacy concerns.

## Intelligent Systems and Responsive Environments

While touring South Korean smart cities, I was struck by the ubiquity of intelligent building management systems, not because they were entirely new or innovative, but because they were so prominently emphasized by smart city managers as essential for urban living. A grandiose metaphor was illustrated in a 2017 Siemens advertisement for its Building Technologies campaign, "Creating Perfect Places." In the ad, the company likened living with intelligent building systems to being in the womb. A sonogram of a child in their mother's womb was overlaid with simple text implying that like the womb, a building outfitted with Siemens's smart building systems is never too cold or warm, never too loud or quiet, and always safe.[10] The intelligent building systems imagined for smart cities by technology vendors are reminiscent of virtual and augmented reality researcher Myron Krueger's concept of "responsive environments" where technologies perceive or sense human behavior and respond with visual or auditory feedback or by making adjustments to environments.[11]

Intelligent building systems aim to create optimized building "performance" and decrease operating costs. Smart building developers claim that these technologies can create more sustainable and enjoyable work and domestic environments: more sustainable due to the building's ability to reallocate space and energy use to counter inefficiencies and manage waste or overuse; more enjoyable due to the customization of spaces and climates according to personal preferences. At present, intelligent building systems (also referred to as smart building systems) that monitor and regulate energy consumption, water recycling, and heating and cooling systems are still emphasized as essential smart city components. Sensors installed throughout a building collect data about energy and water use, lighting and space utilization, and sometimes even occupant location and productivity.[12] Technologies developed as part of these systems include window shades that automatically adjust to changing weather conditions, personalized lighting and room controls, and integrated data systems that process information about all operating systems within an entire building or across multiple buildings. The LEED certification of many smart city buildings is aided by these intelligent building systems and "green" technologies such as pneumatic tubes or vacuums for waste management, charging stations for electric vehicles, smart-card-activated bicycle rental stations, and radio frequency identification sensors on recycling bins to credit users for their deposits. These green systems may be controlled by individual users as well as building managers via wall panels, mobile apps, or smart cards and are linked to centralized control systems that aggregate data about building use and user behaviors.

Several smart cities including Singapore and Vienna are experimenting with smart apartments for elderly citizens. Singapore aims to become a global test bed for aging-in-place technologies such as Smart Elderly Alert Systems that embed wireless panic buttons and sensors in seniors' apartments and Vital Signs Monitoring Systems enabling remote monitoring of blood pressure, glucose levels, and weight.[13] Vienna has created an Active and Assisted Living Test Region (WAALTeR) where 150 senior citizens live in apartments outfitted with digital technologies and wearable devices that monitor their health and promote mobility and good healthcare practices. Aside from tablets, smart watches, cameras, and networked computer systems, apartments also include fall and presence detectors and alarm systems.

In smart cities, rooms, buildings, and streets become responsive through a series of sensors and integrated data systems. Ubiquitous Wi-Fi connectivity, motion and sonic sensor lighting systems and security cameras, on-call autonomous vehicles, and IoT cater to ideals of optimized urban performance and efficiency as key aspects of sustainability and quality of urban life. Instead of merely responding to problems quickly and efficiently, city managers also hope that intelligent systems and big data will predict problems before they occur and inform new service development.

## Internet of Things and Artificial Intelligence

During the first wave of smart city development, technology designers imagined that urban residents would carry a smart card—a wallet-sized microprocessor card encoded with personal information that serves as a passport to smart city systems. A smart card would identify particular users and allow individuals to interact with interconnected urban systems. The same card would be used to unlock your house, turn on personalized climate control and lighting preferences, pay a parking ticket, and

During the first wave of smart city development, technology designers imagined that urban residents would carry a smart card—a wallet-sized microprocessor card encoded with personal information that serves as a passport to smart city systems.

access bike sharing services as well as your medical records. While smart card systems have been critiqued in terms of privacy and security of personal information and data collection, the smart card system speaks to a reiterated vision of smart cities as spaces where everything is connected. IoT underlies and supports this vision. The smart card can be used as a universal passport to the city because high-speed networks connect a variety of services within a centralized system, but also because the physical world is filled with networked objects. Mobile phones and radio frequency identification key fobs often serve as smart cards and connect with QR codes, Bluetooth, and Wi-Fi objects to push or pull real-time information.

IoT is a term used to describe a network in which everyday objects and devices (refrigerators, washing machines, trash cans, floor tiles, coffeemakers, etc.) are connected to the Internet. IoT relies on linking various devices and data sources to a centralized and ubiquitous communication infrastructure, and making data easily accessible to authorities and citizens who can process it to respond to urban activity. This sort of Internet connection allows people and objects as well as objects and other objects to communicate or exchange information with each other over a network. Objects and devices can relay their physical location through GPS and can be encoded with information about their own production. An example often used to illustrate the usefulness of IoT is that of a refrigerator that can call or text a mobile phone to alert residents when they've run out of milk. Other imagined uses of IoT have included alarm clocks that direct coffee-makers to start brewing, mirrors that virtually represent wardrobe options, and GPS sensors embedded in belongings so that you never lose your keys again.

Aside from convenience and efficiency, IoT technologies play a major role in supporting smart city goals of enhancing security and public safety and improving health and sustainability, environmental awareness and responsiveness, and quality of life. In some cases, a single IoT technology may serve all of these functions. For example, smart floor tiles have been developed to harvest energy from footsteps and to sense impact and heat indexes to detect falls and call for help; they can also monitor physical activity within the home for health and security purposes.[14] In other cases, a series of objects connected to Wi-Fi and/or cloud computing systems will interact with each other, the environment, and people around them. For example, LED street lamps in Barcelona receive information about humidity and temperature, pollution, location of nearby pedestrians, and street noise to adjust light levels emitted. A central computer installed in the street allows each lighting unit to communicate with others and manages on-site electric vehicle charging and public Wi-Fi provision. The smart lighting system has been noted to impact public safety, cut electricity and energy costs, and lure people to locations where activities are happening by lighting the street in those areas.

At the municipal level, IoT is understood as fundamental in meeting goals of increased efficiency at lower costs. Telecommunications engineer Andrea Zanella and colleagues describe the implementation of urban IoT as a "win-win situation of increasing the quality and enhancing the services offered to the citizens while bringing an economical advantage for the city administration in terms of the reduction of operational costs."[15] These researchers envision urban IoT as regulating energy consumption in smart buildings; optimizing citywide waste production and collection by installing trash cans that detect weight and reroute garbage collection accordingly; monitoring air quality by connecting joggers' fitness trackers to smart city infrastructure; policing noise through sensors and sound detection algorithms to reduce noise pollution during certain hours; or calling police at the sound of breaking glass or shouting. Many of these technologies already exist. Returning to the case of Barcelona, since 2012 the city has installed sensors that guide drivers to open parking spots and provide digital parking payment options, waste storage and removal systems that eliminate the need for collection vehicles, and noise sensors that have encouraged the city to reduce noise pollution near the popular Plaza del Sol. In partnership with Intel, the city of London has installed sensors and a Wi-Fi network to coordinate

IoT technologies throughout Queen Elizabeth Olympic Park to monitor and report air and water quality, flooding, weather and sunlight, and wildlife. The city plans to use the collected data to better manage the park and park facilities.

## Dashboards and Digital Signage

The smart city is built on sensing, processing, and reporting real-time data about urban activities and making this data accessible to municipal entities and citizens. How data is displayed to the public is often hyped as much as the sensor systems and enhanced infrastructures that collect and process this information. Visualizations of data gathered through sensors or reported through websites or hotlines become integral to the assessment and strategies for optimizing urban performance and infrastructures. If big data about traffic, climate, and energy consumption is meant to change public behavior, then people need to see and understand this data.

The selection of data gathered and displayed on user-friendly smart city dashboards, or user interfaces that organize and visualize information about one or several processes, tends to be structured by ISO 37120, United Nations, or World Health Organization standards for city services and quality of life.[16] Plans and prototypes for smart city dashboard design routinely refer to these standards and global city indicators as best practices for dashboard design that incorporates familiar, overarching themes such as energy, economy, and environment to be measured quantitatively. These indicators are used to identify facts and information to be measured by municipal departments and citizens for governing and managing the city, efforts toward government transparency, and benchmarks to illustrate and track the performance of smart city projects.

Dashboard systems can be useful tools for city managers, municipal departments, and citizens in gaining some insight into urban activities in convenient, low-cost, and legible formats. However, dashboards promote a particular way of knowing the city. These digital aggregations and displays are visual reifications of the totality of systems thinking in urban governance and knowledge. These interfaces account for each system that composes the city in a way that can be measured and statistically analyzed. Rob Kitchin, Theresa Lauriault, and Gavin McArdle, researchers at the National University of Ireland Maynooth, have over 10 years of experience consulting on urban dashboard systems and local and national indicators. They argue that although dashboards purport to collect and display neutral, factual data about the city, these systems reveal tensions between empowerment and accountability, enacting control and policing efficiency.[17] The authors note that data is never "raw" or neutral but always constructed and contextual. They argue that institutionalization and perceived "instrumental rationality" of indicators combined with the act of making them public through dashboards might encourage city managers to manipulate indicators and influence statistics on urban performance or to ignore contradictory forms of urban knowledge and experience.

In addition to sensors and mobile phones, more visible and intentional devices for collecting and displaying information about urban life have proliferated on smart city streets. Nearly all smart cities have dashboards, web portals, and digital signage that display traffic patterns, pollution levels, and information flows within the city. Hypervisible dashboards, digital displays, or kiosks are not only used to help visualize data being collected and processed in smart cities but also to brand or provide evidence of smart city initiatives within public consciousness. In Barcelona, solar panels are installed on bus shelter roofs to power screens that show wait times, and in New York City public pay phones have been remodeled into sleek digital kiosk displays. Through the UrBan Interactions Program (UBI), research groups in Oulu, Finland installed UBI hotspots or interactive public displays that incorporate cameras, RFID readers, Wi-Fi, and high-speed Internet access. Oulu residents and visitors are able to use these screens to access the Internet and information about public transport as well as directories, games, and new media art, and to upload photos and videos.[18] These screens also utilize Bluetooth technology to sense and report information about pedestrian traffic and can be used to push multimedia content to nearby phones. Since many of the functions and infrastructures of the smart city are practically invisible or inaccessible to the public, digital displays of data signify that the smart city exists and is hard at work.

Early incarnations of smart city models emphasized urban projects such as "media walls," "digital odometers," and digital billboards as smart city services. The first public-facing projects in the Digital Media City (DMC) in South Korea emphasized this trend. The Digital Media Street, a main corridor that runs through the district, was slated to include Wi-Fi kiosks that enable Internet access, the Sister Wall (a video wall that displays web cam feeds from Seoul's sister cities), a "location-aware" information delivery system enabling passersby with mobile phones to receive information such as movie listings and coupons relative to their physical location, alongside the Media Board, Digital Odometer, and e-boards. The Media Board incorporated digital signage on building facades to be used by artists as well as for event announcements and advertising. The Digital Odometer diagrammed the amount of data flowing in and out of the city at any given moment through bar graphs and other visualizations. "E-boards," or public kiosks, invited pedestrians to access bus schedules in real time, traffic and neighborhood maps, weather information, and live TV, as well as Internet shopping, chat, and email. Michael Batty and other researchers have critiqued the relatively unstructured visualization of data that appears in projects like the Digital Odometer. He argues that big data streamed from sensors and exhibited on smart city wall displays or dashboards demonstrates that sensor equipment is working rather than providing comprehensive information about wider patterns or systems of urban life.[19] The numerical values, graphs, and percentages displayed may imply a quantitative and holistic understanding of the city but also reinforce the spectacle of smart city data collection rather than useful or meaningful observations.

Digital kiosks that increasingly line city streets are used more like e-boards than digital displays of streaming sensor data. In Kansas City, more than 25 digital kiosks have been installed and display streetcar schedules and buttons to call 911 and 311 alongside advertisements for local restaurants and an events calendar.[20] Approximately 50 10-foot-tall digital kiosks have been contracted in Newark, New Jersey to function as public Internet access points and message boards, to stream advertising and event information, and eventually to collect data about traffic, weather, and possibly facial recognition to detect threats to public safety.[21] Companies such as Intel, IBM, and Nokia and companies specializing in digital kiosk design such as Infinitus and Olea claim that digital kiosks are essential to promoting tourism, increasing retail sales by advertising local businesses, and augmenting citizen engagement by providing free Wi-Fi and access to public services and information while in transit. In some cases, digital kiosks are also read as apparatuses to help ease digital divides by providing Internet and phone access to those without home or mobile phone connection.[22]

## Autonomous Vehicles and Transit Systems

Increasingly, refurbished and "smart" transportation systems have been regarded as integral aspects of smart city development. These physical infrastructures and the electric, carbon-neutral, or autonomous vehicles that move people and goods through cities are often equipped with Wi-Fi and guided by data about traffic patterns and efficient routes. Sensor-monitored and data-driven transportation systems are associated with urban performance in terms of optimizing the movement of people, goods, and services within the city and decreasing congestion; promoting sustainability through reduced carbon emissions and increased options for environmentally friendly travel; and improving public safety through accident reduction and monitoring road conditions. Intelligent and expanded public transit systems have echoed smart city plans for economic development and improved quality of life by promising to connect underserved residents to jobs and social services in more convenient and efficient ways. Transportation development has also been linked to public connectivity more generally, with some municipal officials seeing public transportation as increasing opportunities for public Internet access. For example, in Kansas City, buses and streetcars are equipped with free Wi-Fi connections in an effort to provide ubiquitous public Internet access while collecting data about urban mobility. In Stockholm, the city has installed 4,000 sensors in city streets to track vehicles, bicycles, and traffic patterns. Buses are also equipped with sensors, radio units, and GPS that communicate with traffic signal control systems so that buses running behind schedule (even as little as one minute) automatically receive priority at traffic signals.[23]

In 2016, the US Department of Transportation awarded a Smart City Challenge Grant of $40 million to Columbus, Ohio (with an additional $10 million awarded by Paul G. Allen's Vulcan Inc.). According to the Department of Transportation's press release, Columbus had already raised $90 million to transform its transportation system in line with smart city goals—to "harness the power and potential of data, technology, and creativity to reimagine how people and goods move throughout their city."[24]

Among other innovations, the city pledged to develop infrastructure for three driverless shuttles which would connect a newly constructed transit hub with a retail district to spur economic development and job opportunities.

Autonomous vehicles also serve as a means to collect data about the ways people interact with driverless vehicles and autonomous systems, and possibly more data about urban mobility patterns as pilot systems expand. In 2010, Masdar City deployed a personal rapid transit system consisting of driverless pods for intracity transport. With over 2 million riders in six years (and only two station stops), Masdar City has collected data on how riders interface with driverless systems and promotes the personal rapid transit system as a living laboratory for autonomous vehicle development.[25]

In addition to driverless vehicles, robots have been introduced as solutions to the urban problem of having more laundry or buying more groceries than a person can carry home. Delivery robots—small, autonomous carriers on wheels—are currently being developed and tested for consumer markets by companies in Estonia, Italy, and the United States among other countries.[26] Like autonomous vehicles, these robots support smart city ideals of more pedestrian- and bicycle-friendly spaces and more sustainable and efficient options for short-trip travel. As is the case with other smart city technologies, some urban planners question whether delivery robots actually solve an existing "problem" or whether more advanced technology is a solution at all. As one urban planning professional noted, "Do we seriously have a problem where people can't move stuff down sidewalks? ... I hate to think that excitement over what this technology [robots] could do would displace energy that could be used to employ existing and proven, albeit less exciting, ways to improve our cities."[27]

## Critiques of Smart Technologies

After implementing sensor and IoT technologies, Barcelona's chief technology officer noticed that the city had accumulated immense amounts of data across different platforms. Although data accumulation was the plan from the start, many of the platforms and technologies worked independently of one another, weren't integrated on the same platform, and much of the data collected was not being utilized by city hall or citizens. When city hall realized that employees and department directors weren't utilizing data collected for policy and decision making, they could have decided to limit the amount and type of data collected or selectively gather and analyze data to investigate particular questions about urban systems. Instead, the city decided to open the datasets to the public and install a city-managed, open source sensor network to collect even more data about the city and its citizens.[28]

The solution for obtaining too much unusable data was to collect even more, and to crowdsource labor to find some use for it.

"Big data," or huge amounts of digital information that are collected from a variety of sources and layered or aggregated to produce knowledge, has become the cornerstone of smart cities. As Sarah Brayne explains in her study of policing in Los Angeles, big data has been embraced by a range of organizational actors as a means toward improving efficiency by predicting problems before they occur, allocating resources, and filling informational gaps in analysis.[29] But many of her study participants also expressed that big data and predictive analytics were what organizations felt they *ought* to do in order to be read as legitimate. In many ways, motivations for adopting big data and predictive policing echo reasons for adopting smart city technologies more generally: a combination of the desire to improve efficiency as well as the pressure not to be left behind.

Seeing *more* technology or data as a remedy for issues concerning how to use technology and data reinforces the definition of digital infrastructures and computation as foundations of the smart city. However, many smart city critics also fall into the same sort of technological solutionism as smart city proponents: perhaps the city needs better technologies, or maybe these technologies are being misused. While there is nothing wrong with embracing

"Big data," or huge amounts of digital information that are collected from a variety of sources and layered or aggregated to produce knowledge, has become the cornerstone of smart cities.

technological advancements to potentially improve cities, the folly is believing that data-driven decisions alone will produce socially just urban environments, governance, or resource management.

Cities are heterogeneous, and there is already inequity in them. Smart city technologies don't promise to change power relations, systems of governance, or the politics and priorities of those systems, only how information is gathered, analyzed, and displayed. These technologies are designed for measuring and monitoring, but don't necessarily adjust the ways we can act on the information acquired. If an employee or citizen notices a pattern or problem that needs to be addressed or amended, cities still have to rely on their governing institutions and utility providers to fix it. While smart city technologies might be new, the political, economic, and social contexts in which they are embedded often remain the same. Preexisting power structures and resources still influence (or limit) citizen and government ability, priority, and willingness to act on what is seen in the data.

In addition, the smartness ascribed to technologies suggests that previous systems of decision making, urban management, and governance are inaccurate, inefficient, or unjust. Technologies are seen as apolitical and ideologically neutral entities that can objectively observe and report on rhythms of the city. Smart cities deputize decision making to computers (or to people aided by computers)

Smart city technologies don't promise to change power relations, systems of governance, or the politics and priorities of those systems, only how information is gathered, analyzed, and displayed.

based on the underlying belief that these systems present objective knowledge or evidence to govern the public good. But this is not the case. Digital technologies and the algorithms that process information are never neutral. There is a wealth of literature from science and technology and communication studies that expose and critique the politics of algorithms and their discriminatory outcomes.[30] Even when smart city technology designers and planners carefully consider harms and risks to communities or environments, there may be unintended consequences and privacy violations. Furthermore, data accumulation and transparency do not automatically make governments more effective and responsive.[31] Since many smart city initiatives are top-down designs by governments and/or corporations, entrenched institutional actors are often able to control and leverage new technologies and datasets to inform or promote existing interests.

Smart city initiatives in Chicago provide a revealing example of both the prowess and the limits of smart technology's influence. Chicago's Array of Things, myriad open data initiatives, and carefully constructed smart city roadmaps have been extolled by smart city developers. The municipal government collects and publishes copious amounts of data about the city that can be accessed by citizens online and downloaded in machine-readable formats for free. Mayor Rahm Emanuel's open data executive order declared Chicago's commitment to "creating an unprecedented level of transparency, honesty and accountability to the public in City government" through publication and citizen interaction with public data.[32] By 2017, the CIO claimed that Chicago provided 600 interactive datasets to citizens through its open data portal and credited predictive analytics as a successful method for regulating public health (rodent control, West Nile virus outbreaks, restaurant inspections) and public utilities (flooding, sewer, and storm water management).[33] However, the city's 2012 open data mandate did not change the public perception of Chicago's city hall and police force as corrupt, dysfunctional, and discriminatory; and even with a pledge of transparency on the books, the mayor's office attempted to withhold surveillance video from citizens.[34] While the influx of sensors and available datasets may affect the provision of public services and create the illusion or performance of transparency, smart technologies did not significantly alter relationships and hierarchies within urban power structures.

As Keller Easterling notes, there are disjunctures between the stories and promises associated with urban infrastructures and what the city is actually doing.[35] Additionally, there are often disjunctures between data collected and what cities can change through the acquisition and use of that data. In discussions with city government officials and CIOs, I've found that executives lack a concrete vision for how collecting data about urban space or activities might be actionable or fulfill a municipal or community goal. I've asked Cisco representatives in Songdo, New York, and Kansas City the same questions: your company offers many urban "solutions," but what are the problems you're trying to solve? How will collecting and analyzing this data help you solve particular problems? There are rarely any clear answers to these questions. Representatives repeat the same blanket challenges of urban growth—overpopulation, pollution, traffic congestion and inefficient mobility, climate change, waste management—and evade questions about what specific information they're hoping to find. City executives and CIOs proudly quantify the amount and variety of datasets collected but describe a diagnostic treasure hunt at the center of big data analysis and invite citizens to do the same: take a look under the hood and see what you find. Ever-expanding surveillance and sensing capabilities reify the practice of "seeing what you find" as well. Professor of sociology and anthropology Orit Halpern and colleagues suggest that perhaps smart cities foster expertise and increased faith in "techniques of calculability" and mitigating uncertainty rather than investigating and attempting to solve urban issues or citizens' concerns.[36] From this perspective, smart cities are brimming with the spectacle of endless data methodologies, and little else.

A key aspect of urban life that is underestimated in smart city technology design and implementation is the process by which some external stimulus provides a linkage between people and prompts strangers to talk to one another.[37] Instead promotional materials, demo spaces, and vision statements by smart city planners present the opposite: digital kiosks for individual use; data and information accessed through smart phones, individual monitors, or in private spaces; virtual walls as home consumer goods. Smart technologies hail urban populations as individual end users with personalized, data-driven needs. Although alternative uses exist, software like dashboards, city platforms, and apps function as concierge services that position citizens as consumers or clients rather than community members or collaborators in the production of the city as place. While some of the technologies imagined for these spaces arguably improve spatial relations in terms of safety, efficiency, and sustainability (with respect to traffic, parking, energy consumption, and water recycling for example), the corporations that distribute these technologies envision minimal feedback and interaction between the city and the citizen.

As I've discussed elsewhere, top-down smart cities express a particular vision of ubiquitous computing that deemphasizes the agency and role of people and communities in the use of technologies, depriviliging their knowledge and experience of urban life within digital activities.[38] Instead of attention toward community needs and civic engagement, there is a focus on infrastructure, efficiency, and automation in smart city projects. As a result, these projects generally forsake any emphasis on ICTs that encourage communication, community formation, and civic engagement in favor of activities focused on navigation and optimized movement, information relay, and advertisements.

In the majority of examples described in this chapter, technologies work to connect people with computers or digital information, not to connect people with other people or with user-generated knowledge about the city as place. Information about urban environments transmitted through digital kiosks and smart city apps is equivalent to information accessible from any Internet-connected mobile phone or municipal website: weather, traffic, bus schedules, etc. While such environmental information is useful, the absence of interpersonal interaction or interaction with the city as an inhabited place is important to note. However, as will be discussed in chapter 4, other uses and opportunities exist for these smart city technologies, and are emerging in cities that claim to be smart.

## Conclusion

Many of the problems identified by smart city technology vendors are issues that resonate across the history of urbanization: crime and public safety, congestion and traffic, pollution and climate control. These issues persist because they are not easily solved or managed. Thinking that new technologies or gathering more or bigger datasets alone can address these basic, timeless questions is naïve at best. Relying on technologies to be "smart" might lead to reforms that don't genuinely change urban governance or may yield limited, temporary, or shortsighted improvements to the quality of public service delivery. In addition, these technological solutions might not garner legitimacy, engagement, or salience among members of the public. Algorithms, big data, and AI may change how and what decisions are made, but not the underlying apparatus and sociopolitical infrastructures that support and carry out these decisions or whom these decisions benefit the most.

The intentions and imaginations of technology designers shape but do not determine technology use. However, the affordances and assumptions designed into smart city technologies and the contexts in which they are expected to be used reveal limited understandings of how people choose to interact with urban space and each other. There are alternatives to the scenarios envisioned and promoted by smart city technology purveyors, in which cities and local communities utilize social media and real-time data for storm and crisis communication (e.g., Resilient NYC) or residents use municipally owned open data to navigate zoning laws and shape investments in affordable housing or transit routes (e.g., Los Angeles's WebCode by re:code LA; Austin's Corridor Housing Preservation Tool). Some researchers, community members, and technology designers actively question current models for smart technology and push back on dominant smart city visions that undermine the desires and agency of people in the street. The following chapters analyze the presence and positioning of people in smart city plans and reflect on the ways in which smart city technologies and initiatives can be re-envisioned as spaces where citizens claim and act on their digital right to the city.

# CITIZEN INPUT AND ENGAGEMENT

In Hollands's frequently referenced critique, the sociologist highlights a major conflict within smart city conception and implementation: the mismatch between promoting transnational ICT industries and managerial elites and serving ordinary citizens. Smart city political critiques build on this tension, emphasizing the detriment of supporting top-down innovation and governance at the expense of grassroots needs, behaviors, and regulations. Several authors suggest that focusing on corporate technologies and master plans necessarily excludes or neglects social justice, equality, and inclusion issues in the name of profit.[1] These strategies foster cities and technologies that improve lives of elites while maintaining or furthering gaps among urban poor and those lacking digital literacy and access. If citizens are considered at all, critics argue, their role in creating the city, expressing their experiences or desires, or having input into smart city infrastructures and technologies is limited.

In promotional and research materials, at conferences and summits, and in digital roadmaps, industry and municipal executives discuss the necessity of citizen engagement in smart city development and use. However, the concepts of citizen engagement and participation take on particular meanings within these market-driven conversations. This chapter analyzes how smart-from-the-start, retrofitted, and social city developers envision citizen participation in smart cities. Depending on whom you ask, the citizen's role in smart cities is either a highly contested topic, an integral force for urban improvement, or an afterthought. To begin, I investigate these themes by synthesizing some critiques of smart cities as nondemocratic, top-down enterprises that ignore or exclude citizen engagement. Smart city developers are very conscious of these critiques and of the negative impacts offered by top-down approaches to urban development and technology design. The chapter concludes with a discussion of alternate and emerging perspectives on "smart citizens" or grassroots efforts toward citizen participation in smart cities, and how people use digital technologies to collaboratively solve issues that affect their cities and their lives.

## Citizen Engagement in Smart Cities

### Where Are the People?

A principal critique of smart cities in regard to citizen engagement and participation is that there is none. The market-driven models sold and readily adopted in cities around the world share a technological solutionist view that largely ignores sociality and placemaking within cities. For centuries, urban theorists have argued that we build cities to commune with other people, generate culture, and strengthen our communities.[2] Smart city developments sideline these attributes and view cities as places to erect buildings and infrastructures that generate wealth for a select few.[3] People, their needs, and their agency to coproduce urban space tend to be unheeded or absent in dominant smart city models, though these claim to improve quality of life. When people are included in smart city plans, they are imagined as individual data generators, urban lifestyle and technology consumers, or the cause of urban problems.

An awkward discourse about citizens emerges in smart city promotional materials. CIOs and municipal officials express concern that citizens aren't adequately engaged in smart city development. These concerns generally reference a lack of resident attendance at smart city demos, a general malaise or lack of enthusiasm for smart

When people are included in smart city plans, they are imagined as individual data generators, urban lifestyle and technology consumers, or the cause of urban problems.

city initiatives, or a feeling that citizens aren't "at the same level of readiness as their cities are."[4]

Frequently, people's habits and desires are seen as impeding smart city initiatives. When asked about challenges to smart city development, a managing director for an IoT consultancy bluntly stated: "First of all, those pesky people living in cities makes it difficult to retrofit smart city solutions because you can't just ask people to leave town while you implement solutions that might impact their lives."[5] The director's comments are reflected in other technology companies' perspectives. At a smart cities event, an engineer joked that IBM "tends to look at the pipes and then people come along and destroy all our nice optimized systems."[6] In another instance, Guruduth Banavar, vice president and CTO of global public-sector business at IBM, noted that a recurring issue with building smart cities is that there are significant challenges in "getting citizens fully engaged in all transformations that take place."[7] Instead of trying to engage a wide range or representative group of citizens, the IBM executive claimed that "the hallmark of a smart city is having the right people, in the right numbers, working the technology in the right way."[8] At a recent event in Kansas City, Chelsea Collier from Digi.City and Smart City Connect reflected on the importance of "people" and the "people doing great things" in smart cities. It quickly became evident that "people" referred to city leaders who embrace dominant smart city concepts and technologies, and not the general public. These quotes imply that although smart cities rhetoric emphasizes citizen participation, the participatory processes envisioned are not generally inclusive, nor do their executors perceive average residents as providing much value or input into the systems they're creating. This perspective privileges expert and top-down design and decision-making processes over more variegated models and power dynamics.

People are seen as potential problems for smart city developers because of the dynamic informality and messiness of their interactions and desires. Instead of supporting citizen interactions and participation, smart cities formalize urban sociality in ways that work against cities' informal character. Dominant smart city models try to simplify and straighten out the messiness and dynamism of everyday urban life though digital media, replacing certain types of complexity (traffic jams) with others (big data about traffic jams).[9] Aside from difficulties in attracting people to efficient but not culturally vibrant places, there are other significant smart city problems: notably the problem of placing people as central to the city and designing technologies and physical places that benefit local communities. The following sections elaborate on these issues.

**People Lack Agency**

In my discussions with corporate executives and industry consultants, no phrase is repeated more often than the claim that smart cities will "improve quality of life"; how and for whom are never fully articulated. What is clear is that citizens don't decide what this means. My research into master plans and promotional documents for smart-from-the-start cities indicates that people and social behaviors are framed by developers as "bugs" in the system. People resemble urban problems that need to be managed and regulated: they move and consume inefficiently, get lost, lose track of their children and belongings, cause crime and public safety hazards, and need computation to help them function. People are envisioned as other types of "bugs" too: drosophila for testing new initiatives within testbed cities; worker ants busily producing data and expected to "work on" themselves and their behaviors.[10]

People become users or customers rather than citizens or producers of the city—they're not part of the ecosystem but interact with it. Citizens lack agency in their ability to create or change improvements within smart cities. Technological systems often measure "sectors and agencies" (e.g., municipal departments and infrastructures, public and private utility providers and services) rather than actions people take to improve neighborhoods and communities.[11] De Lange and de Waal also note that the "triple helix" of smart city projects—municipal governments, universities or research institutes, and technology industries and entrepreneurs—ignore citizen roles as agents or actors. Instead, these entities rely on mutual expertise to guide and create change within cities and make informed decisions about smart city structure and functionality. Seeing citizens as end users or customers for smart city products and services delimits and neglects their agency as participants in smart city design and development.

Additionally, proposed smart city technologies actually inhibit decision-making practices of people on the street. Because smart city systems encourage flow, they disrupt spaces of dwelling, pause, and casual encounters that take place there—no waiting for the bus or for the street light to change, no lingering, no getting lost. Autonomous vehicles and automated traffic lights limit human decisions and engagement with traffic flow. Sensor-based street and building lights turn on and off without our help. Cameras track and report our whereabouts without our consent to entities not of our choosing. AI and IoT offer valet services that outsource information retrieval and data analysis and push algorithmically determined recommendations to our phones, while dashboards and apps present already analyzed and curated data for the purpose of making "informed" decisions. Streamlining and optimizing cities for efficiency and convenience often means limiting debate and interaction among citizens and between citizens and the city.

Because smart city systems encourage flow, they disrupt spaces of dwelling, pause, and casual encounters that take place there—no waiting for the bus or for the street light to change, no lingering, no getting lost.

Smart city technologies position citizens as passive recipients and information providers of automated data, while the data changes their behaviors in a rational manner. In many cases, citizen participation is reduced to uploading heart rates and photographs of potholes with little or no chance of altering institutions and urban processes or deliberating with one another. Interacting with city services and information in this way contrasts with the fact that people routinely use digital media in opposite ways—for collective intelligence and networked interactions, communing, and creative expression.

Catherine Mulligan, a researcher and expert in cybersecurity and digital economies, argues that within smart city development, corporate and municipal actors haven't stopped to ask what citizens want.[12] Although much more ethnographic and qualitative research in this area is needed from universities and community organizers, corporate and municipal actors do attempt to engage urban residents in smart city discussions. Several US cities that have launched large-scale smart city initiatives established meetings, events, and online forums to reach out to citizens about smart city plans. Invitations to participate in smart city planning through public information sessions, meetups, or online forums are often extended. However, these opportunities tend to feel largely performative and perfunctory rather than productive, and they only engage select urban populations. While smart city executives publicly recognize that people are central to vibrant cities, they don't make substantive efforts to incorporate a wide range of resident voices into smart city development.

**People Are Excluded from Smart City Conversations**
The general public is largely excluded from smart city development in a variety of ways. Decisions about programming and technology design and implementation for smart-from-the-start cities have occurred solidly behind corporate and government doors. Discussions and debates about smart city initiatives are generally treated as elite conversations among expert stakeholders such as technology designers and researchers, corporate and municipal executives, entrepreneurs, and government employees. Smart city summits, expos, and conferences where concepts, directions for initiatives, and technology development are discussed charge attendees hundreds of dollars (sometimes over $1,000) in registration fees.

When smart city developers attempt to be inclusive through participatory planning processes, they may be relying on inadequate models. Best practices for participatory planning are commonly critiqued for excluding perspectives representative of larger urban communities, and participatory planning outcomes aren't necessarily incorporated into final plans or practices. Several scholars observe that in participatory or codesign models, citizens are only involved in infrastructure projects "downstream," or their input becomes inconsequential.[13]

Cultural geographers Anthony McLean, Harriet Bulkeley, and Mike Crang have identified a cycle of citizen engagement in smart city infrastructure planning. Cities cultivated as smart technology experimental spaces and test beds defer citizen collaboration to the final stages of infrastructure implementation.[14] Once infrastructure is deployed, citizens are invited to use technologies and publicly share their data while policymakers delegate responsibilities for utilizing this data back to urban citizens. Relatedly, digital culture anthropologist Dorien Zandbergen notes that European policymakers embrace and emphasize versions of urban cocreation or DIY citizen data science in smart city rhetoric. However, her ethnographic study of a participatory air sensor project found tensions between corporate and citizen interests, including the fact that decisions regarding platform design and project branding were made by corporate participants without citizen input.[15]

The Smart City Council's Readiness Guide encourages developers to engage in participatory planning and in hybrid bottom-up and top-down decision-making and innovation processes. The guide refers to technology companies like Oracle and Amey as experts on how to incorporate participatory planning and engage communities, and warns of several risks involved when engaging citizens in smart city development. The authors note that dealing with people is complicated and that their solutions to urban problems might be motivated by self-interest. Ironically, the same could be said of the corporations influencing the readiness guide. The guide also mentions that lower-income communities are often excluded from smart city conversations, but no quoted experts offer ways to engage or empower these populations to act on their concerns.

I have found that periods of public input for smart city planning are socially and temporally limited, occurring for brief periods via social media, online forums, or during happy hours for local tech entrepreneurs. In Kansas City, smart city meetups and town hall meetings were announced via email, Twitter, and Facebook sometimes earlier on the day they were scheduled to occur. While some of these events focused on digital inclusion, people without Internet access wouldn't have been able to receive an invitation. Although open to the public, these informal meetings started at 4 or 5 pm and were located far from lower-income neighborhoods. Held at cocktail or craft beer bars, boutique coffee shops, and followed by hors d'oeuvres in gentrified areas or arts districts, they were likely to exclude people who didn't work or live nearby, didn't work 9–5 pm, or felt out of place in artisanal bars or cafés. Technology company and startup employees were always in attendance as were local entrepreneurs and mayor's office employees. Everyone seemed to know each other, and after attending a few of these events, I noticed that there were barely any unfamiliar faces.

The conversations occurring in these spaces between "community partners" such as startup and incubator directors and regulars at smart city, innovation, tech industry, and cabinet meetings were sometimes live-tweeted, but information presented at these events was rarely distributed otherwise. All photos and tweets documenting these discussions resembled public relations hype, the photos showing smiling or intrigued faces of attendees and people networking or drinking locally produced beer, the tweets celebrating the "great conversations" happening without actually reporting the content of these discussions.

After the first meetup, concerned residents pointed out a lack of people of color in attendance as evidenced by event photos posted online. A few Kansas City residents of color and those outside of the local tech scene tweeted messages indicating that they hadn't known about the smart city gathering and information sessions but would have liked to attend. Kansas City community members requested to be notified of future events, and some lamented that they were not able to attend due to work schedules. Although these tweets were "liked" or bookmarked by a few participants and organizers, they generally went unanswered.[16]

On the other hand, free-of-charge and public smart city demos in Kansas City were not well attended. In coordination with the public streetcar service launch (a project developed as part of Kansas City's smart city initiative), the city hosted a demo space called "Smart City Village" along the route. Located in a glass-windowed exhibition space in the downtown business district, it featured a few booths with representatives from Cisco, Sensity (responsive and data-driven lighting system), and the streetcar initiative displaying their wares. When I visited on a sunny Saturday afternoon, I was the only person in attendance.

## Smart City Planners' Perspectives on Citizen Engagement

Smart city guides routinely urge developers to "engage" citizens. According to planning documents and public statements, smart city developers understand that citizens are integral to the success and sustainability of smart cities. Many of these reports and roadmaps note the importance of connecting all citizens and neighborhoods with broadband infrastructure and smart technologies, and of developing "solutions" that "deliver value" for residents. The Smart City World Expo 2017 report (where the conference theme was "Empower Cities, Empower

People") warns municipal planners that involving citizens in smart city development is often the most difficult challenge, but a necessary one. The report recommends harnessing the productive power of citizens to aid in city management through living labs where citizens test technologies.[17] "Empower" is a vague catchphrase that is repeated but never defined and is used to support a range of public-facing initiatives: open data systems, apps and dashboards, digitized information and services (311, license applications, government websites, etc.). Any occasion at which citizens are given information about their activities collected by sensors or surveillance cameras is noted as "empowering people."

This image of technological empowerment is also articulated in funding proposals. In promotional materials for smart city challenges, building an "inclusive" city is often listed as a requirement for application. Several finalists for the US Department of Transportation Challenge Grant mentioned citizen lives as foundational to their projects, and all city proposals mentioned improving connections with underserved and minority communities as central to their narrative. Kansas City wanted to empower citizens by collecting more data about them; Austin proposed to engage underserved communities to understand their needs; Portland pledged to ensure access to new transportation options and include community members as integral to developing smart technologies; Columbus noted how smart corridors and payment systems would improve infant mortality rates in underserved communities.[18] Although rhetoric around inclusion and engaging marginalized communities has noticeably increased, the discussion of community and citizen engagement among corporate partners takes three dominant forms. Citizen engagement is generally envisioned in terms of customer service, crowdsourced conversations, or access to big datasets.

## Customer Service

For many smart city advocates, citizen engagement is presented in retail terms in which citizens are envisioned as customers for municipal and private services. Smart city development goals are framed as optimizing delivery of "citizen services" such as transportation, utility provision, snow and trash removal, and public safety. Additionally, cities mention the importance of virtually connecting citizens to businesses to streamline connections between residents and storefronts they frequent. In both cases, citizen interactions mimic customer service exchanges.

Since the inception of its smart city efforts, New York has focused on multimodal outlets for accessing information or filing a complaint with the city. Live chat, 311 online, and social media to identify and report electrical outages are examples of "platforms for complaining" which have become commonplace in smart city citizen engagement

For many smart city advocates, citizen engagement is presented in retail terms in which citizens are envisioned as customers for municipal and private services.

efforts. Other services such as FixMyStreet, SeeClickFix, BOS:311, and Commonwealth Connect, where mobile phone users send photos of potholes to maintenance operations, are part of a customer service interpretation of citizen engagement. New York describes its 311 online and social media efforts as a "streamlined customer service experience" where citizens are engaged as consumers of public utility services who make demands of service providers. As Dietmar Offenhuber, professor of design and public policy, explains, these user-friendly, cookie-cutter and minimalist versions of citizen participation that focus on reporting service provision can obscure larger systematic issues and opportunities. For example, Offenhuber notes that while reporting potholes and being notified of their repair may make citizens feel that their requests are being responded to, these "incremental fixes can come at the expense of more comprehensive solutions such as using a road surface that is less prone to potholes."[19] In addition, these modes of citizen engagement often reflect personal desires rather than community activism and rarely translate to other forms of citizen empowerment or participation.

## Crowdsourced Conversations

In addition to customer service frameworks, citizen engagement is understood as interacting with city officials, departments, or other citizens in discussions online.

Inviting people to participate on city-operated accounts, newsfeeds, or discussion boards allows the city to listen to and collect data about citizen perspectives. Conventionally, the invitation is to "participate" in, but not necessarily control, initiate, or lead, conversations about urban environments. Although social media can be used as a tool for citizens to converse and deliberate with one another, smart city initiatives often invest in conversations started by government accounts resembling a broadcast model where mayors or city representatives post to audiences or practice delegated listening.[20]

In many cases, but definitely not all, citizens are positioned as audiences for city government interaction rather than as voices to be listened to. New York's smart city campaigns illustrate this relationship. The digital roadmap lists 12 goals for citizen engagement, the majority of which involve launching live chat, Facebook, Tumblr, Twitter, YouTube, and Foursquare city-operated accounts. Municipal presence on social media was proposed to push information and notifications to citizens quickly, promote municipal events and place-branding, and hear citizens' needs and experiences. While these social media accounts garnered numerous followers, they mostly receive "likes" or retweets rather than comments or conversations and are driven by posts from municipal representatives. Facebook community interaction and support groups are hosted on pages where city representatives moderate conversations and maintain sole control over the content of the main posts (see NYC Quits Smoking and NYC Schools, for example). However, the city claims that these outlets foster community-led discussion, with government employees only playing a supporting role.[21]

Typically, cities follow established marketing and public relations practices regarding audience interaction, such as posting audio/visual content, posing questions at the end of posts, and using hashtags to direct and aggregate responses. Overall, cities create architectures of participation for user-generated content without critically examining how corporate platforms and industry models of engagement are conceptualized and implemented. For example, social media use for civic or neighborhood coordination and communication can be understood as exclusive by some urban populations. Residents may be reluctant to use Facebook and Twitter for neighborhood communication as they could exclude several neighbors (particularly elderly, lower-income, and less digitally literate).[22] Participants asked for input into New York's digital roadmap echoed these sentiments. Respondents noted that social media and emerging technologies are not accessible to all and therefore should be used cautiously by the city. Residents stated that the primary response to solving urban problems shouldn't be "we need an iPhone app!" or "let's use Twitter!" because not everyone uses social media and not everyone has a smartphone.[23]

Overall, cities create architectures of participation for user-generated content without critically examining how corporate platforms and industry models of engagement are conceptualized and implemented.

Municipal officials also regard crowdfunding and crowdsourcing platforms as useful for citizen engagement. Platforms such as Neighbor.ly, EveryBlock, Neighborland, Brickstarter, Kickstarter, and YIMBY have all been recommended as applications for gaining insight into citizen perspectives. However, the types of perspectives shared and by whom are rarely questioned and are often inaccurately utilized as representative samples of urban populations. Companies like Oracle have encouraged smart cities to harness the wisdom of crowds for economic development and innovation but remind potential clients that harnessing the value of crowds does not mean relinquishing control to people. Instead, "corporate IT has a critical role to play in every collaborative business model."[24] As this statement implies, crowdsourcing is perceived as an activity that shouldn't be wholly allocated to the crowd but orchestrated and leveraged by corporate or municipal entities.

Building trust and relationships between government and members of the public doesn't happen through privacy policies alone or discussions around technologies that are meant to control citizen behavior and foster efficiency. After conducting interviews with civic media practitioners in major US cities and people who use media to promote democratic processes, civic media scholars and designers Eric Gordon and Gabriel Mugar argued that to build trust and relationships with citizens, civic media users need to build networks, maintain spaces for open discussion and continual input, and distribute ownership.[25] The researchers offer an interpretation of civic media that necessarily demotes the end goals of efficiency and optimization in favor of "meaningful inefficiencies" that favor connection and reflection—the opposite of dominant smart city trends.

In contrast to corporate-driven models, some cities have developed and employed platforms focused on creating networks of trust, collaboration, and participation by connecting citizens to one another and to local government to accomplish shared goals. Better Reykjavik is one example of a grassroots ideation or open innovation platform that allows citizens to propose, collaboratively revise, and upvote policy initiatives before they are submitted to the municipal government. In London, the mayor's office collaborated with local startup Spacehive to produce a municipal crowdfunding platform ("Mayor's Crowdfunding Pilot") where neighbors, local entrepreneurs, and urban developers could propose and jointly fund neighborhood improvement initiatives. Similar to crowdfunding platforms like Kickstarter, if enough people supported an idea then the project moved forward. In this version, the mayor's office contributed funds to a select subset of crowdfunded projects based on feasibility, innovation, and amount of local support. In its first year, the Mayor's Crowdfunding Pilot raised £830,000 for 35 projects with

2,300 backers (rising to over 50 projects by the end of the pilot program).[26] The City of London provided a platform where citizen-led neighborhood improvement initiatives could start locally, address meaningful issues and places, and foster a mutual sense of empowerment and ownership between fellow citizens and the city.

## Data and Public Engagement

Citizen engagement efforts involving data collection and user-generated content have brought attention to ethical issues and citizen concerns regarding privacy and surveillance. Processes and policies for collecting and analyzing big data have come under scrutiny in smart city development particularly. For example, the main privacy advisor for Sidewalk Labs' Toronto waterfront, Ann Cavoukian, resigned over the fact that data gathered from populations living and moving through the smart city district would be identifiable and available to third-party companies not bound to Sidewalk Labs' privacy protection agreements. Several other domain experts commissioned for the project have also resigned due to issues of transparency, privacy, and accountability around data protection. One of these experts, Saadia Muzaffar, founder of Tech Girls Canada, noted that Google had a "blatant disregard for resident concerns about data and digital infrastructure," as well as "apathy and a lack of leadership regarding shaky public trust."[27]

In terms of knowledge produced through big data practices and platforms, researchers have identified how algorithmic systems and big data use by public institutions potentially reproduce inequalities and generate risks to racial minorities, disadvantaged populations, and the neighborhoods in which they live.[28] As discussed below, when collected and used ethically and in coordination with community needs and infrastructures for public engagement, crowdsourced content, big data, and open data can be utilized to benefit urban environments and residents.

## Smart Citizens and Alternative Perspectives

Recognition of "smart citizens" rather than smart cities gained visibility after several smart-from-the-start cities had broken ground. The focus on smart citizens is presented as both a critique and an alternative to corporate smart city development. Smart citizens are already all around us: using smartphones and social media to connect with each other, navigate, and experience the city in innovative and informed ways.[29] Some scholars and planners suggest that smart citizens need to be cultivated,[30] while other critiques draw attention to the fact that "smart" isn't inherently linked to digital media use; citizens are smart even when they don't use technologies to accomplish goals, and smart cities should be designed with this reality in mind. Arab Spring protests and subsequent movements utilizing smartphones and/or social media for mobilization are commonly presented as exemplary smart citizen actions. However, smart citizen discourse also relies on technology use in moderation or when appropriate to encourage thoughtful, active citizens who make decisions about urban life and urban activities.[31] Designers should reconsider how to best harness this intelligence, not coopt or deter it.[32]

Several manifestos for the smart citizen present criteria, desires, or calls for smart citizenship.[33] Recognizing and cultivating smart citizens instead of, or in addition to, smart cities is seen as a way to counter top-down approaches of real estate developers, municipal governments, and technology companies. Approaching smart citizens as foundations for smart cities recognizes citizen agency in addressing issues that governments and their tech partners attempt to ameliorate. This perspective reenvisions smart cities as spaces of collective intelligence and collaboration where people work together to address concerns beyond efficient services, such as education systems, poverty, housing, as well as ideas and issues generated from urban communities.

Smart citizen perspectives highlight the importance of community or grassroots organization and participation models in smart city development. Researchers suggest that citizens be consulted during design, development, implementation, and use phases of smart city and technology design. Smart citizens are informed about the technologies being implemented in their cities, and inform and decide how they will be used and how they will impact their lives. These citizens understand the basics of privacy, technological affordances, and data analysis and are able to engage in debates about smart city development. In this vein, if smart cities were actually "smart" then planning processes would adopt democratic or grassroots approaches and connect marginalized populations with ICTs to enhance their access to employment markets, education, health, and social cohesion.

Alternative smart cities approaches rely on distinct conceptions of what makes a city "smart" and what citizens' and community roles should be. Smart citizen engagement strategies are designed and/or owned by communities and begin with questions and community members' needs rather than the agendas of corporations or municipal governments. Some of these efforts repurpose top-down development plans and corporate technologies; others might collect similar types of data as corporations and governments but create community control and ownership of that data. These initiatives still rely on technology as a way to be "smart," but recognize sociality, stewardship, social cohesion, and grassroots cooperation as central to a city's structure and emotional connections to place.

## Open Data beyond "Hackathons"

Various agents in smart city development embrace citizen-generated data as free and open, not privatized or proprietary. Some grassroots or smart citizen initiatives attempt to create more accessible, anonymized data commons and data sharing that are localized, customizable, and publicly owned. A current trend in open data led by city governments is to host datasets through municipal sites that can be downloaded and utilized by residents and third-party developers to create civic applications and services. This data is presented and used at hackathons hosted by municipalities to encourage residents, local entrepreneurs, and technology designers to incorporate city data into civic media projects. Another emerging trend organizes neighborhoods to decide what information they want to collect and how they want to use that information.

Social cities proponents and other critics of dominant smart city paradigms have called for shifts in models and constraints on data access. At present, open data initiatives have become commonplace. However, these initiatives offer packaged, cleaned, and curated access to data in the form of alerts or advisories, and only provide statistics and information from institutionalized or official channels of data collection such as censuses or government departments. Open data and e-governance initiatives tend to benefit administrators who want to observe and control citizen behavior with(in) infrastructure systems and services. In contrast, this same data can be harnessed and used by citizens in different ways: to raise issues of equity in distribution and access to resources, question social power, and address institutionalized disadvantages. For example, Beth Simone Noveck, professor and former director of the White House Open Government Initiative, describes open data and open government as a means to open up institutional decision making to systematic and ongoing deliberation and collaboration with diverse citizenry, with an emphasis on soliciting and utilizing public feedback and expertise.[34]

A key goal for digital data commons and open data systems is to increase accessibility, community awareness, and participation in city government and urban life. Within data-driven smart cities, open datasets are framed as a means toward these goals. In addition to privacy and security issues, a concern about the logic behind open data initiatives is that the collection and exhibition of datasets about urban activities and populations may become a proxy for the voice of the people within civic government and urban planning. Professors of media and communications Nick Couldry and Alison Powell have noted "voice" as an essential value for democratic and social organization through which publics give accounts of themselves and their everyday lives.[35] Couldry and Powell also argue that the automatic generation and aggregation of data, which becomes the backbone of dominant smart city visions, exists in direct contrast to valuing public voices. They suggest that transparency of data and methods of data collection, instead of listening to people's accounts of urban experience, is framed as a way for municipal government to remain accountable to the publics they serve.

Alternative models for community awareness and engagement are also on the rise within open government and open innovation systems. Mobile, decentralized emergency and disaster response systems such as PulsePoint, Ushahidi, and Resilient NYC enable members of the public to serve as first responders. Crowdsourcing initiatives that encourage collaboration between the public and city government beyond data provision or hacking, particularly around participatory budgeting, have become more commonplace. Researchers and community organizers have suggested listening tours as a way for municipal officials to connect with community members and to develop planning strategies in consultation with citizens (see Beta NYC for one example). Expanding what counts as data and valid data sources about the city or what facts and information are included in open datasets could value a wider range of urban knowledge and experience and invite diverse communities to share, collect, and analyze their experiences. Some examples might include more qualitative datasets such as interviews and oral histories, volunteered social media check-ins or posts, neighborhood surveys, or community-made media and storytelling.

In his book *Smart Cities*, Townsend is optimistic about cities that maintain subsidized or community-owned networks, embrace "computational leadership networks," and encourage civic hackers' socially minded tinkering. He mentions Foursquare's API workshops and DIYcity's hackathons as examples of how open data and participatory cultures of collaboration lead to urban innovation and problem solving. Quite often, the data utilized by civic hackers through hackathons or sponsored workshops is determined by government organizations or private companies that collect and make it available. However, there are examples of community stakeholders' early involvement in open data initiatives where citizens determine the data and indicators used to monitor the city.[36] One example is the City Monitor, a set of indicators collectively developed by municipal government officials and employees, citizens, and researchers used to measure the performance of at least 13 Flemish cities.[37]

In contexts beyond hackathons, actionable knowledge about the city can be cocreated by communities and government organizations to encourage conversations and collaborative problem solving around shared urban issues. Sarah Williams, Director of the Civic Data Design Lab at MIT, believes that "big data will not change the world unless it is collected and synthesized into tools that have a public benefit."[38] Her work illustrates how various urban communities can be involved in the identification, aggregation, and analysis of urban data, how data visualizations can lead to policy change, and how these processes can empower communities as decision makers with shared interests in improving their city. Her lab's big data visualizations regarding lack of reentry programs in Brooklyn, New York influenced the introduction of the Criminal Justice Reinvestment Act of 2010, which allocated $25 million to reentry for previously incarcerated Americans. Purpose Labs offers another example of how visualizations and open data can lead to potential policy changes and public attention to urban issues. In its BreathLife campaign, Purpose developed a series of interactive data visualizations and social media content informing citizens in 52 cities about air quality in their area and actions they can take to support policies that reduce health and environmental impacts of air pollution.[39]

In another inspiring example, Williams discussed how the codesign of new data visualization and collection tools can enable communities to tell their own stories, where community perspectives are leveraged to instruct governments about their needs. Working with matatu drivers (private minibuses that serve as primary forms of transportation in Nairobi, Kenya), researchers, students and technology designers, and Civic Data Design Lab members helped residents create and edit a map of informal travel networks through Nairobi.[40] Previously, maps of matatu routes and stops hadn't existed, which meant that city transit networks weren't readily legible to drivers, riders, and government officials, potentially affecting efficiency and gaps in service. The Digital Matatus project designed apps, open maps, and datasets about matatu activity, and experimented with processes of community engagement and data collection around informal transportation networks. Instead of trying to replace informal or semiformal transportation networks with high-tech vehicles or vendor-driven services, Digital Matatus innovated methods of citizen and government engagement in aggregating and utilizing information about already existing networks and modes of urban mobility. Team members generated new tools, processes of collaboration, and methods for involving multiple stakeholders throughout all stages of data gathering and planning processes.

## Repurposing Technologies and Data Collection

Smart technology critics argue that citizens would do better with raw materials rather than finished products. Instead of relying on corporate technologies and prepackaged data, alternative approaches urge local technologists, community organizations, and city governments to develop their own digital tools for civic engagement.

Advocates for this perspective urge city governments and citizens to provide local residents with training and/or support to develop their own technologies and DIY crowdsourced information, data collection, and organized collective action. UNESCO offers one example of such community-focused connectivity efforts. Instead of relying on city, state, or corporate efforts to build telecommunications and Internet access points, UNESCO issued a Community Telecenter Cookbook for Africa that provides instructions to communities for building their own telecommunications center. This approach allocates and recognizes citizen agency as problem solver and coproducer of smart city initiatives.

In Detroit, the Allied Media Project and Open Technology Institute launched the Detroit Digital Stewards Program that instructs community members and organizers on designing and deploying wireless mesh networks in their neighborhoods.[41] The program has extended its training beyond Detroit to include communities in Washington, New York, Sayada (Tunisia), and Dharamsala (India). The sense of stewardship and citizen collaboration in building community-designed and -owned communications infrastructures has provided low-cost digital connectivity and fostered a sense of pride in place, efficacy to solve urban problems, and augmented digital inclusion through grassroots initiatives.

Researchers and technology designers have also re-purposed smart technologies. Media design labs such as MIT's Senseable City Lab have experimented with alternate uses of sensors in urban space. Projects such as Trash Track place sensors on discarded objects like coffee cups to track progress within trash and recycling systems. Other projects provide commuters with real-time, open datasets that indicate efficient routes home or neighborhood-specific strategies to reduce energy consumption and manage waste (LIVE Singapore).

Designers have tried to shift power hierarchies by putting smart technologies (such as sensors, cameras, and data aggregation) in the hands of marginalized urban communities. In Detroit, university researchers trained teenagers to use sensor kits and design surveys to track air quality, heat and humidity, and traffic along the nearby riverfront. The project, Sensors in a Shoebox, transmits data collected to a public Twitter account so that community members with social media access can view and download data and monitor their neighborhood environment over time.[42] Putting sensors in the hands of underprivileged teens, teaching them to use these technologies, and asking and answering questions about their environment through data collection and analysis familiarizes residents with methods for sensor and data use by ordinary citizens. Other nongovernmental organizations focus on educating publics about the value of data collection and analysis.

Mapping for Change trains disadvantaged communities and local organizations to collect and map data and develop initiatives around sustainability and environmental concerns such as noise, odor pollution, and air quality as well as transportation, accessibility, and mobility issues. These initiatives encourage citizens to investigate and make data-informed decisions about significant local concerns on their own, which shifts agency and responsibility for improving local conditions and quality of life to the hands of individuals and communities. Projects that resemble Mapping for Change are categorized as "citizen science" or participatory action research, in which projects are developed and conducted by citizens in collaboration with researchers and use scientific methods to address pressing issues and provide public access to information about these issues.

Collaborative and participatory media use is another grassroots strategy for cultivating smart city and smart citizen initiatives. Quotidian examples of utilizing smartphones for collaborative coordination can be seen in services like Waze for monitoring traffic, Uber for ride sharing, or Task Rabbit for crowdsourcing labor. Moving beyond these for-profit models, projects such as Map Kibera (a citizen mapping project in Kenya) and the mobile phone app Onde Tem Tiroteio (Where the Shootouts Are) that crowdsources information and notifies people of violent incidents in Rio de Janeiro illustrate how urban residents are willing to adopt digital tools and collectively produce data to improve public safety and sense of place. Other citizen sensing projects weave smart city initiatives and data collection into mundane habits and routines using hardware and software like mobile phones and apps or introducing wearable sensors into routine activities like walking or driving. In Paris, pedestrians were outfitted with climate and ozone sensors to monitor air pollution levels, while other cities attempt to activate mobile phones as sensors that monitor traffic patterns and environmental conditions. However, the use of mobile phones as both sensing and communication devices can be extended to encourage interaction with fellow citizens and the shared data they're collecting.

Smart city efforts that meet citizens on their turf by engaging preexisting activities or technology use, utilizing technologies people already feel comfortable with, or codesigning efforts that require new digital literacies and training have shown sustained and active participation from residents over time. Efforts that have immediate and direct effects on community-identified needs and quality of life also tend to encourage continued citizen engagement. Grassroots projects that encourage citizens to connect with other people, institutions, or resources to solve urban problems encourage a sense of ownership, stewardship, and efficacy within urban space and governance. In contrast to smart city visions promoted by IBM,

Rio's citizens created an alternative, grassroots smart city network. Alessandra Orofino and Miguel Lago cofounded Meu Rio in 2011 as a digital space for residents to initiate campaigns and mobilize for urban causes important to them. Over 160,000 citizens ages 20–29 have already joined the platform and yielded successful citizen mobilization efforts. A young girl saved her school from being razed to accommodate a parking lot for Olympics visitors; a favela resident created a recycling project for his neighborhood; and a mother of a missing daughter mobilized 15,000 people to pressure local government to establish a police unit investigating missing persons cases.[43] The citizen participation project has expanded to other cities throughout Brazil under the title Nossas or "Ours." The name of the network speaks to the sense of ownership over the initiatives, the issues being identified and addressed (collective concerns that urban residents have identified themselves), and a public reminder of shared rights to the city—that residents have the right and agency to change, manage, redesign, and care for cities.

As these examples illustrate, collaborative data collection and analysis or citizen-led mobilization serve as ways to engage various urban communities and stakeholders and foster collaboration between citizens and municipalities. This work highlights needs for data and technology literacy programs alongside open data and citizen mobilization initiatives. Research examples from the Civic

Data Design Lab reinforce the perspective that data literacy, and not just the availability of data, benefits publics and urban improvement. In the case of the matatu map, citizen involvement in the project recognized residents' unique knowledge of how the city worked while making processes of gathering, analyzing, and visualizing datasets more legible. Citizens' data literacy and urban knowledge enabled their engagement with grassroots as well as top-down smart city efforts.

## Conclusion

Smart city developers often struggle to map smart city promises, rhetoric, and symbolic power onto local needs, social affordances, and experiences of urban space. While some scholars and designers suggest data collection and analysis can improve community opportunities for collective action, critics argue that contemporary smart cities don't even pretend to adequately address citizen needs and agency. As examples in this chapter illustrate, it is possible and advantageous to plan smart cities that consider actually existing places, populations, and their concerns as central to urban development, as opposed to planning for the internal needs of institutions and government agencies. Even the corporate smart city would look and feel very different if it were being marketed to citizens rather than municipal governments.

Emerging perspectives for empowering smart citizens illustrate how dominant smart city models are more adept at measuring places than at fostering democratic processes or offering useful tools for meaningful social interactions. In their current form, smart cities build technical networks and institutional, customer service modes for citizen connection to city services. Dominant smart city models project promises of comfort and convenience for some (but not all) citizens and suggest that sociability and the interactions and needs of "those pesky people" are problems that need to be solved.

Corporate smart-from-the-start and retrofitted city models focus on amenities rather than meaningful use. By prioritizing top-down goals and visions, smart city planners struggle with how to put people first.[44] In terms of citizen engagement and participation, smart city developers circulate both limited visions and constant calls for more citizen participation and engagement. Social cities and smart citizen perspectives challenge designers to think deeper about cities and what people do with(in) them, not just the data that might come from their activities.

From attending smart city expos and conferences and speaking with CIOs, city managers, and smart city technology vendors, it seems that many powerful smart city decision makers have become more interested in data collection and use than in what questions to ask about this data or the purposes for gathering it. This view of data as objective facts to be collected and technologies as ideologically neutral entities to be implemented encourages a functionalist view of the city as a place. Smart city developers could stand to think more profoundly about the methods, goals, and biases embedded in the networks and software they implement and how innovative digital technologies can facilitate democratic processes and grassroots innovation, involving a range of citizen voices throughout smart city planning processes. Smart cities have the potential to celebrate the coproduction and collaborative nature of cities, but they have to begin to see this role as more productive than infrastructure and service optimization.

# FUTURE DIRECTIONS FOR SMART CITIES

In this book I've highlighted some social, political, and economic opportunities and tensions at work in current conceptions of smart cities. Smart cities are regarded by several researchers and planners as neoliberal spaces shaped by corporate technology vendors in the service of top-down urban governance and efficient management strategies. Others view ICT implementation and smart city efforts as rendering urban environments more resilient, responsive, and sustainable in terms of resource allocation, public service provision, and quality of life. Some scholars suggest smart cities result from privatization and entrepreneurial shifts in urban governance that disenfranchise or devalue citizen agency and control in shaping cities. Researchers and planners have developed sociotechnical strategies for mobilizing urban residents and using data for public benefits. But smart cities convey additional tensions between promises of decentralized power and information ascribed to digital media and the centralization of power and decision making in technology design and implementation in dominant smart city models.

"Smart city" has become an industry buzzword proposing a digitized, data-driven future for urban governance and urban life in which efficiency is privileged above other values and processes. However, this is not the only vision for meaningful technology use and sustainable growth in urban spaces. The concept and power dynamics around smart city development are continually being revised and expanded but also need to be detached from corporate trademarks and trajectories.

Some smart city project executives have even renounced the term based on its negative connotation. Rohit Aggarwala, director of urban policy implementation at Sidewalk Labs, rejected "smart city" as a descriptor for Google's Toronto megaproject. He told a reporter that the term is "too closely associated with software products focused on wringing maximum efficiency out of cash-strapped city services."[1] Harvard law professor and former White House advisor Susan Crawford and recognized government management expert Stephen Goldsmith suggest that we think of cities using ICTs to empower municipal leaders and citizens as "responsive" rather than "smart."[2] Perhaps terms like "connected city," "networked city," "collaborative city," "resilient city," or prefixes that signify other values and outcomes cities hope to achieve would serve as better signifiers.

Proponents of revising smart city paradigms do not propose that we abandon the idea of networked or digitally connected cities completely; far from it. For example, some critics have suggested that we learn how to work with corporate smart city vendors in more mutually and universally beneficial ways while critically interrogating their visions, plans, and practices. To do this, citizens, municipal officials, corporate leaders, and advocacy groups need to educate themselves about how technologies work, how citizens and democratic citizenship work, and power and access issues that radiate throughout these relationships.

Such views are not anti-technology, but they are against technological solutionism and hope to develop new perspectives on what networked cities are or could be. Ideally, networked city design and development will provide new opportunities to reexamine urban systems and institutions, address inequities or social justice issues within those systems, and generate inclusive debates and input about improving these issues. It is necessary to recognize opportunities for digital infrastructures to benefit disadvantaged communities, as well as risks and harms to these populations. Tools for data collection and analysis can then be repositioned within contexts for fostering collective action and community mobilization, and can actually be implemented to support and improve people's lives.

Ethan Zuckerman, Director of the Center for Civic Media at MIT, suggests that civic media need to operate within the "insurrectionist" mode rather than in support of sedimented and staid institutional values. The same could be said of smart cities. Dominant smart city visions are governed by institutional priorities reliant on market capitalism and public administration. Shifting from institutional values such as efficiency and cost-effectiveness toward decentralized, localized, or grassroots interpretations of urban needs and social justice invites different modes of innovation and reinvention in smart city development. Instead of being an end in themselves, smart cities could provide opportunities to question and renegotiate institutional values, finding middle ground where institutions and citizens can mutually benefit and grow.

In this brief conclusion, I summarize some emerging philosophies on smart city futures and identify potential areas for further research on this topic. Future directions for smart city development (drawing on examples and debates presented in this book) include democratizing connected cities, recognizing citizen placemaking efforts, and developing sociotechnical methods that foster collaboration across urban stakeholders and prioritize values beyond efficiency and entrepreneurship.

## Democratizing Connected Cities

All smart city interpretations emphasize some form of networking, communication, and responsiveness. Instead of thinking of the city as "smart," we can think of it as networked or connected and the relationships that make it so. If the city is a network, then its production and organization are neither top-down nor bottom-up but distributed and shared. Shifts in how smart city planners, citizens, and municipal officials think about connectivity and participation can generate a sense of co-ownership of urban space and foster an ability to act in collaborative ways.

Smart city designers have gestured toward collective ways of producing urban space, but tend to fall back on top-down, universalized models of urban governance in which centralized control, speed, and efficiency are valued over democracy. Smart city plans are too often initiated without contributions, critique, and consent of the people they purport to serve. Practices that democratize urban planning such as participatory planning have been embraced by smart city strategists, but these strategists often engage communities after decisions about smart city infrastructure, technologies, and roadmaps have already been contracted. While urban planning literature has provided some models for public participation in planning, these studies also illustrate circumscribed effects of citizen participation and limited numbers and diversity

All smart city interpretations emphasize some form of networking, communication, and responsiveness. Instead of thinking of the city as "smart," we can think of it as networked or connected and the relationships that make it so.

of participants involved. It is rare for city governments to give people a chance to evaluate and vote on smart city initiatives or to coauthor digital roadmaps. However, anyone who has lived in or studied cities can point to repeated examples of communities and neighborhoods demanding more control over their own existence and urban future.

Putting people first in smart city design and implementation means that designers and developers understand lived relationships between people, place, and urban infrastructures while ethically and earnestly listening and attending to citizens' needs. As suggested in chapter 4, smart city developers need to generate more social or sociotechnical solutions that foster collaboration between diverse stakeholders, and in particular to learn from and engage urban populations that have historically experienced differential power and agency over urban environments and systems. Populations heavily and regularly surveilled by government entities might have insightful suggestions and critiques concerning data ethics and the types of information gathering used to make decisions about urban space and services.

Smart city development teams routinely struggle with educating, informing, and collaborating with community members. Developing and standardizing new methods for citizen dialogue and collaboration from the outset is imperative. As a bookend, finding ways to continue and

act on these conversations could hold smart city developers accountable to citizens and support sustainable urban
growth. These methods do not displace cost-efficient
technologies that aid urban governance and management,
but utilize these same technologies and infrastructures to
foster trust and civic involvement among urban inhabitants. Infrastructures that encourage dialogue between
stakeholders, allocate resources and public services more
efficiently and equitably, and reinvest in urban improvement might not involve ICTs at all. Instead of interpreting
"smartness" and progress through technological implementation or entrepreneurship, we could reframe connected cities as spaces that value social infrastructures as
means toward resilience, responsiveness, and sustainable
growth.

I have identified ways in which technology design
and use are highly centralized and dictated by selective
assumptions held by smart city vendors. Smart city technologies emphasize vertical structures of surveillance and
data collection where preexisting power dynamics and
governance methods are reinscribed and amplified in digital form. Community-initiated and participatory media
projects could encourage citizens to monitor institutions
that govern urban space and social relations. Although
there are some instances of sousveillance in projects such
as EveryBlock and Oakland Crimespotting, for example,
traditional smart city models don't offer ample space for

citizens to authoritatively monitor government entities and power structures, only some of the services that they provide.

Smart cities are "internally differentiated," which means that some urban places, people, and activities will be privileged over others.[3] An early illustration of this unequal access to smart infrastructure is urban broadband networks in which certain populations and neighborhoods are imagined as part of networked cities while others are unintentionally excluded. While top-down urban broadband and free public Wi-Fi projects aim to ameliorate digital divides, they also tend to reinscribe or heighten preexisting social and economic gaps and access to infrastructure. In reaction, neighborhoods all over the world have installed and managed their own Internet mesh networks, set up computer labs, repurposed or hacked preexisting telecommunication networks, and created digital literacy programs. These participatory and citizen-led examples illustrate the need to expand notions of who smart city stakeholders are and how they can contribute to and critique urban development.

Furthermore, cities need to expand notions of what counts as "data" and where and to whom municipal governments, researchers, and communities turn to understand cities. The tenets of data feminism provide a starting point for critiquing and revising dominant ways of producing actionable knowledge about cities, how this knowledge is communicated and visualized, and whose perspectives are included or marginalized.

Civic media and data visualization scholars Catherine D'Ignazio and Lauren Klein propose that theories and methods from the humanities should inform practices of data collection, visualization, and design to recognize potential for pluralism in knowledge production.[4] In terms of stakeholder diversity and community involvement, D'Ignazio and Klein suggest that data visualizations should actively reflect the positionality and background of the design team and imagined users in order to identify and include omitted or marginalized perspectives. These suggested practices of reflecting on power dynamics and on perspectives represented and fostering an ethics of inclusive coproduction with user communities are excellent starting points for efforts to democratize smart city planning and operations.

## Re-Placeing the Smart City

Models for developing and implementing smart city plans should be questioned and critiqued by those who build and manage them to evaluate resonance and usefulness for particular urban environments and communities. Smart city developers construct places in exclusive ways that invite those who are already networked and recognized as politically and socially powerful to participate. Instead of being open for interrogation, these plans are often presented as inexorable, one-size-fits-all visions for urban space. Networked or connected cities could benefit from being horizontal, localized, and dispersed, with more raw materials provided to local communities to make or demand changes within their neighborhoods. Actors interested in fostering connected cities need to recognize ongoing placemaking efforts by local populations and how these efforts can become foundations for smart city plans instead of being completely refashioned.

Relying on systems that transcode urban activities and human behavior into data is limiting in terms of understanding cities as diverse fields of care. These systems position algorithms and data analysts as imperative to unlocking the meaning of cities and recommending how cities should be run. In addition to computational methods for understanding urban environments, domain experts from social sciences, humanities, community organizations, and social welfare need seats at planning tables. The functionalist view of cities currently maintained by many smart city developers needs to shift toward more context-sensitive and human-centered approaches to designing public spaces. Instead of emphasizing universal urban experiences, smart city designers could directly consider the different, interrelated urban communities living and working together and value the friction, flexibility, and serendipity in these differences. Moving forward, smart city developers need to reconsider their assumptions and basic understandings of contemporary cities and what people do in them, not just the data that might come from their production.

Dominant smart city models have much to learn from feminist geography and theories of placemaking in their approach to organizing urban space. Feminist geographic theories focus on rhythms and routines of everyday life, inequity and difference, and identity in shaping public and private experiences within urban spaces. Unlike smart city executives, feminist geographers consider people as creative, active agents who have capacities to change the meaning of urban plans and built environments.[5] They focus on the work people do to make sense of their environments, rather than being passive recipients of top-down articulations of space. Feminist urban planning scholarship has focused on addressing exclusionary decision-making practices that devalue women and minority input and experiences and critique policies and planning practices that reinforce inequities or embrace neoliberal or corporatist visions of urban life.[6]

These alternative perspectives directly address blind spots in smart city visions and development plans. Feminist critiques of urban space and urban planning identify how neoliberal and corporate interventions limit public participation and civic engagement in the social life and

Dominant smart city models have much to learn from feminist geography and theories of placemaking in their approach to organizing urban space. Feminist geographic theories focus on rhythms and routines of everyday life, inequity and difference, and identity in shaping public and private experiences within urban spaces.

equitable and sustainable growth of cities. A key suggestion for future research and development would be to ask and explore questions regarding what an inclusive or feminist smart city would look and feel like, or what methods could be employed toward this design. I offer a few starting points below.

**Suggestions and Future Directions**

Smart city developers need to work closely with local communities to understand their preexisting relationships to urban place and realize the limits of "technological fixes." A first step is recognizing that technology alone will not fundamentally transform urban governance or necessarily improve quality of life for all residents. It is important to realize that technology and smart city master plans are never ideologically neutral and might be significantly more harmful to some populations than to others. Technological solutions are not wholly capable of fixing underlying conditions that lead to urban inequalities and inadequate service provision. Relatedly, municipal officials need to consider whether institutionalized systems and people's behaviors actually change when provided with information about urban activities. Can big data or open data really change urban behavior? And should it?

Several smart city critiques include a quote from Cedric Price: "Technology is the answer. But what is the question?"[7] Citizens, government, and public-sector representatives can work together at the outset to generate questions and problems before data is collected. In many cases, additional or advanced technology adoption may be an appropriate response. However, smart city endeavors focused on building trust or sense of ownership through ongoing community interactions might lead to more robust and sustainable innovation and problem solving. If data is collected and used to suggest changes to urban behavior and activity, then citizens should have full access to the collection processes and outcomes of this data. Ideas about data use in terms of privacy, social justice, ethics, and purpose need to be continually reevaluated by city government and urban inhabitants. Reevaluating the purpose of data collection and analysis within smart cities to focus on process rather than outcomes might create more spaces for citizen collaboration and input. For example, using data collection and visualizations to initiate conversations about urban issues and concerns rather than conclude or ameliorate them is an alternative vision for big data use in smart cities.

Encouraging and listening to online and offline tactical urbanism and community improvement projects is particularly important to smart city development, as these projects reveal needs and desires of citizens and their proposed methods for addressing shared issues. Support and recognition of community-initiated projects invite innovation, efficacy, and feelings of belonging to the city. These projects evidence what can and might be done if communities were provided raw materials and funding to contribute to connected cities on their own terms. Recognizing citizen problem-solving efforts celebrates rather than smooths over meaningful inefficiencies and democratic processes.

Design thinking favoring ideals such as connectivity, intersectionality, and reflection (adapted from Gordon and Mugar) rather than speed and optimization shifts smart city priorities and values from infrastructure and efficiency toward actual needs of people on the ground. Concerns about justice and privilege should also take center stage. Utilizing local and university expertise more holistically by inviting sociologists, anthropologists, and humanists into smart city conversations alongside engineers, computer scientists, and business professors could aid in understanding lived urban experiences as more than just quantitative data.

We need to widen perspectives on how digital media can and should be used in cities and whether "smart cities" are helpful at all. Municipal officials should consider at what point in decision-making and planning processes citizens are invited to provide input into smart city plans. In soliciting public feedback or recruiting citizen

Design thinking favoring ideals such as connectivity, intersectionality, and reflection rather than speed and optimization shifts smart city priorities and values from infrastructure and efficiency toward actual needs of people on the ground.

collaborators, further investment in equitable forms of invitation, meeting times and locations, and representative sets of skills and knowledge can engage more inclusive samples of community members. In lieu of performative gestures toward citizen participation, a genuine focus on collective responsibility and equity is needed. Reaching out to disadvantaged or marginalized populations might mean traveling to or hosting smart city and urban planning events in trusted spaces and neighborhoods where these residents live and providing communities with necessary literacies to understand smart city efforts that are being proposed.

For populations to engage in discussions and debates about smart city design and development, they need access to tools for spatial and digital literacy and information about city government decision-making processes. While grants and awards are given to cities eager to develop corporate smart cities, these foundations and granting agencies could prioritize citizen education, public digital and spatial literacy programs, funding for research about urban experiences, or developing participatory planning opportunities for diverse urban communities.

In terms of future directions for smart city research, there needs to be more ethnographic and qualitative work from universities, nonprofits, and community organizations about what people want from connected cities. We need to find better methods for engaging in democratic collaborations around the future of our cities. Less affluent or digitally literate communities are routinely and unnecessarily left out of smart city conversations. Although municipal leaders reiterate the importance of citizen engagement, there are relatively few models for empowering populations to act on their concerns. Research into innovative participatory planning models and improved methods for collaborating with low-income and marginalized communities about urban development and infrastructures would benefit smart city development and city governance more generally. Researchers and citizens also need to continue developing tactics for holding municipalities accountable in utilizing information gathered through participatory smart city efforts in meaningful and just ways.

Along with the spaces themselves, "smart city" terminology and values are under construction. Researchers, planners, technology designers, and citizens worldwide are producing alternatives to corporate models of smart city design and implementation. But we need more. There are many things a city could be other than "smart." As people who live in cities or are concerned about their future, it's our responsibility and in our best interest to identify and cultivate these other options.

# GLOSSARY

**Big data**
Massive amounts of digital information collected from a variety of sources and layered or aggregated to understand patterns, associations, or interactions.

**Chief information officer (CIO)**
Senior member of city administration hired by the mayor's office to direct and advocate for technology implementation and policy. A chief technology officer (CTO), chief innovation officer, or chief digital strategist may have the same responsibilities as a CIO under a different title.

**Citizen engagement**
Ongoing active, direct interactions between citizens and public decision makers and institutions. Typically these take the form of feedback or dialogue between public institutions and citizens that affects decisions or policy outcomes.

**City in a box**
Term used to describe and critique corporate one-size-fits-all master plans sold to cities. These packages consist of a la carte technologies with specialized foci to be mixed and matched in constructing piecemeal smart city strategies.

**Dashboard**
User interface that organizes and visualizes information about one or several processes in user-friendly or readable formats.

**Free economic zone**
Site or region designated by a national government as exempt from standard taxes and/or other economic regulations to spur economic activity and attract investment.

**Internet of things (IoT)**
Phrase used to describe a network of devices, including everyday objects and appliances (such as refrigerators, washing machines, trash cans), that are connected to the Internet, allowing people and objects as well as objects and other objects to communicate or exchange information.

**Neoliberalism**
Set of beliefs that prioritize economic and ideological foundations of market capitalism (e.g., competition, entrepreneurialism, privatization, and deregulation) and extend these tenets to structure aspects of public and private worlds and interactions.

**Open data**
Data intended to be freely available and accessible and to be used, repurposed, and redistributed by anyone.

**Predictive analytics**
The use of algorithms and machine learning to identify the likelihood of a future occurrence based on analysis of previously collected data.

**Public-private partnerships (PPPs)**
Contractual agreements between federal, state, or local agencies (public sector) and for-profit organizations or corporations (private sector).

**Retrofitted city**
Term used by industry and municipal executives to describe a preexisting city that incorporates digital infrastructure, data collection and analysis, or other smart city technologies to drive urban governance and management and respond to and influence urban activities.

**Sensor**
A device that detects physical properties or phenomena like lights, motion, or sound and records and transmits observed environmental changes to other devices.

**Smart citizen**
Alternate conceptualization in which citizens are central to the design and function of cities and use open, decentralized, and/or customized corporate technologies in the service of collectively improving and maintaining their cities and communities.

**Smart city**
Prospect for managing urban space that aggressively implements digital technologies to collect a range of data about the city that can be used to make

decisions about how to regulate city services and activities and influence citizen behavior.

**Smart city "solutions"**
Corporate term for technologies that gather and process information about people, data, and resources and report this information to centralized systems or authorities.

**Smart-from-the-start city**
A city built from the ground up with digital technologies, infrastructure, data gathering, and analytics as integral aspects of its master plan.

**Social city**
Vision of the city in which people use technologies to engage with the city and each other: to actively influence or change their environment, to cultivate a sense of place and belonging in the city, and to communicate, collaborate, and build relationships with other urban residents and organizations.

**Technological solutionism**
Belief that any problem or difficulty can be solved through the prescription and use of technology.

# NOTES

**Chapter 1**

1. "A Grand but Last Hurrah," *The Advertiser* (Adelaide), October 29, 1996.

2. Robert G. Hollands, "Will the Real Smart City Please Stand Up?," *City* 12, no. 3 (2008): 303–320.

3. Ola Söderström, Till Paasche, and Francisco Klauser, "Smart Cities as Corporate Storytelling," *City* 18, no. 3 (2014): 307–320.

4. Antoine Picon, *Smart Cities: A Spatialised Intelligence* (West Sussex, UK: John Wiley & Sons, 2015).

5. Ibid.

6. Jay Forrester, *Urban Dynamics* (Portland, OR: Productivity Press, 1969).

7. Jay Forrester, "The Beginning of System Dynamics" (Stuttgart, Germany, 1989); Louis Edward Alfeld, "Urban Dynamics—The First Fifty Years," *System Dynamics Review* 11, no. 3 (Fall 1995): 199–217.

8. John R. Logan and Harvey L. Molotch, *Urban Fortunes: The Political Economy of Place* (Berkeley: University of California Press, 1987); Taylor Shelton, Matthew Zook, and Alan Wiig, "The 'Actually Existing Smart City,'" *Cambridge Journal of Regions, Economy and Society* 8, no. 1 (March 1, 2015): 13–25.

9. Vito Albino, Umberto Berardi, and Rosa Maria Dangelico, "Smart Cities: Definitions, Dimensions, Performance, and Initiatives," *Journal of Urban Technology* 22, no. 1 (January 2015): 3–21.

10. Anthony M. Townsend, *Smart Cities: Big Data, Civic Hackers, and the Quest for a New Utopia* (New York: W. W. Norton, 2013), xii.

11. "Advantech, Intel Plan for Smart Cities and the Internet of Things," *Control* 26, no. 12 (December 18, 2013): 24–26.

12. Aaron Back, "IBM Launches a 'Smart City' Project in China," *Wall Street Journal*, Eastern Edition, September 17, 2009, sec. Technology.

13. Natasha Singer, "I.B.M. Takes 'Smarter Cities' Concept to Rio de Janeiro," *New York Times*, March 3, 2012, sec. Business Day.

14. Söderström, Paasche, and Klauser, "Smart Cities as Corporate Storytelling."

15. Leonidas Anthopoulos, *Understanding Smart Cities: A Tool for Smart Government or an Industrial Trick?* (Cham, Switzerland: Springer International, 2017).

16. Söderström, Paasche, and Klauser, "Smart Cities as Corporate Storytelling."

17. Edgar Pieterse, *City Futures: Confronting the Crisis of Urban Development* (Chicago: University of Chicago Press, 2008), 79.

18. Robert G. Hollands, "Critical Interventions into the Corporate Smart City," *Cambridge Journal of Regions, Economy and Society* 8, no. 1 (March 1, 2015): 61–77.

19. Rob Kitchin, "Making Sense of Smart Cities: Addressing Present Short-comings," *Cambridge Journal of Regions, Economy and Society* 8, no. 1 (March 1, 2015): 131–136.

20. Adam Greenfield, *Against the Smart City*, 1.3 edition (Do projects, 2013).

21. Shannon Mattern, "A City Is Not a Computer," *Places Journal*, February 7, 2017.

22. Siemens, "Smart Cities: Trends," Pictures of the Future, June 7, 2015, https://www.siemens.com/innovation/en/home/pictures-of-the-future/infrastructure-and-finance/smart-cities-trends.html.

23. For example see danah boyd and Kate Crawford, "Critical Questions for Big Data," *Information Communication and Society* 15, no. 5 (2012): 662–679.

24. Shelton, Zook, and Wiig, "The 'Actually Existing Smart City.'"

25. Taewoo Nam and Theresa A. Pardo, "Conceptualizing Smart City with Dimensions of Technology, People, and Institutions," in *The Proceedings of the 12th Annual International Conference on Digital Government Research* (College Park, MD: ACM, 2011), 284.

26. Mike Steep and Marzieh Nabi, "Smart Cities Improve the Health of Their Citizens," *Forbes*, June 27, 2016.

27. Helen Knight, "The City with a Brain," *New Scientist* 208, no. 2781 (October 9, 2010): 22–23.

28. Masdar, "About Masdar City," 2016, http://www.masdar.ae/en/masdar-city/detail/one-of-the-worlds-most-sustainable-communities-masdar-city-is-an-emerging-g.

29. "Siemens—Smart Cities," accessed February 25, 2017, http://w3.siemens.com/topics/global/en/sustainable-cities/Documents/smart-cities-en/index.html#/en/infos/detail.

30. Anna Kordunsky, "Overcoming the Sustainability Challenge: An Inter-view with Guruduth Banavar," *Journal of International Affairs* 65, no. 2 (Spring/Summer 2012): 147–153.

31. Robin Meadows, "San Francisco and Paris Get Smart," *Frontiers in Ecology and the Environment* 11, no. 4 (2013): 172; Kordunsky, "Overcoming the Sustainability Challenge."

32. Sofia Shwayri, "From the New Town to the Ubiquitous Ecocity: A Korean New Urban Type?," *Traditional Dwellings and Settlements Review* 26 (2014):

79–80; Nadine Post, "Developer Makes Big Waves With World's 'Smartest' Eco-City." *ENR: Engineering News-Record* 268, no. 2 (January, 23 2012): 42.

33. Valeria Saiu, "The Three Pitfalls of Sustainable City: A Conceptual Framework for Evaluating the Theory-Practice Gap," *Sustainability* 9, no. 12 (2017).

34. US Department of Transportation, "Smart City Challenge," September 28, 2016, https://www.transportation.gov/smartcity.

35. Ibid., 12.

36. Nick Taylor Buck and Aidan While, "Competitive Urbanism and the Limits to Smart City Innovation: The UK Future Cities Initiative," *Urban Studies*, August 5, 2015.

37. Jesse Berst, "How to Guarantee a Win from the Smart Cities Council Readiness Challenge Grants," Smart Cities Council, November 3, 2016. http://smartcitiescouncil.com/article/how-guarantee-win-smart-cities -council-readiness-challenge-grants.

38. European Commission, Strategic Energy Technologies Information System, "European Initiative on Smart Cities," accessed February 27, 2017, https://setis.ec.europa.eu/set-plan-implementation/technology-roadmaps/ european-initiative-smart-cities.

39. S. P. Mohanty, U. Choppali, and E. Kougianos, "Everything You Wanted to Know about Smart Cities: The Internet of Things Is the Backbone," *IEEE Consumer Electronics Magazine* 5, no. 3 (July 2016): 60–70.

40. The full list of categories includes: economy, education, energy, environment and climate change, finance, governance, health, housing, population and social conditions, recreation, safety, solid waste, sport and culture, telecommunication, transportation, urban/local agriculture and food security, urban planning, waste water, and water.

41. Andrea Caragliu, Chiara Del Bo, and Peter Nijkamp, "Smart Cities in Europe," *Journal of Urban Technology* 18, no. 2 (April 2011): 65–82.

## Chapter 2

1. Aditi Shah, "India Builds First 'Smart' City as Urban Population Swells," *Reuters*, April 15, 2015; Abhishek Lodha and Subbu Narayanswamy, "Creating a 'Smart City' from the Ground up in India," McKinsey & Company, January 2017, https://www.mckinsey.com/industries/capital-projects-and -infrastructure/our-insights/creating-a-smart-city-from-the-ground-up-in -india; PTI, "China Has Highest Number of Smart City Pilot Projects: Report," *Economic Times*, February 20, 2018, sec. World News; Jamil Anderlini,

"China's Next 'City from Scratch' Called into Question," *Financial Times*, June 7, 2017.

2. The Next Silicon Valley, "DISCOVER: Gramercy District, the USA's Smart City in a Box—The Next Silicon Valley," *The Next Silicon Valley* (blog), April 22, 2017. http://www.thenextsiliconvalley.com/2017/04/22/3210discover -gramercy-district-the-usas-smart-city-in-a-box/.

3. Sidewalk Toronto, "New District in Toronto Will Tackle the Challenges of Urban Growth," Sidewalk Labs, October 17, 2017, www.sidewalktoronto.ca.

4. Finbarr Toesland, "Smart-from-the-Start Cities: The Way Forward," *Raconteur*, March 30, 2016, https://www.raconteur.net/technology/smart-from -the-start-cities-is-the-way-forward.

5. Dan Hill, "Essay: On the Smart City; Or, a 'Manifesto' for Smart Citizens Instead," *cityofsound*, February 2013, http://www.cityofsound.com/blog/ 2013/02/on-the-smart-city-a-call-for-smart-citizens-instead.html.

6. Eric Jaffe, "How Are Those Cities of the Future Coming Along?," CityLab, September 11, 2013, http://www.theatlanticcities.com/technology/2013/09/ how-are-those-cities-future-coming-along/6855/.

7. Greg Lindsay, "Cisco's Big Bet on New Songdo: Creating Cities from Scratch," *Fast Company*, February 2010.

8. Keller Easterling, "The Zone," in *Visionary Power: Producing the Contemporary City*, ed. Christine De Baan, Joachim Declerck, and Véronique Patteeuw (Rotterdam: NAi Publishers, 2007), 75.

9. Ibid.

10. Incheon Free Economic Zone Authority, "IFEZ Project Handbook: We Build on Success," Public Relations Office of Incheon Free Economic Zone Authority, Incheon, Korea, December 2011.

11. Masdar City, "Masdar City Free Zone: Become a Masdar City Client," Masdar Free Zone, 2013, http://www.masdarcityfreezone.com/why-masdar/ benefits.

12. Souvanic Roy, "The Smart City Paradigm in India: Issues and Challenges of Sustainability and Inclusiveness," *Social Scientist* 44, no. 5/6 (2016): 29–48.

13. Taylor Shelton, Matthew Zook, and Alan Wiig, "The 'Actually Existing Smart City,'" *Cambridge Journal of Regions, Economy and Society* 8, no. 1 (March 1, 2015): 13–25.

14. Jesse Berst, "How to Guarantee a Win from the Smart Cities Council Readiness Challenge Grants," Smart Cities Council, November 3, 2016. http://smartcitiescouncil.com/article/how-guarantee-win-smart-cities -council-readiness-challenge-grants.

15. Ayona Datta, "What Is Smart about Smart Cities? A Response from the Global South," *The City Inside Out* (blog), June 30, 2013, https://ayonadatta .com/2013/06/smart-cities-global-south/.

16. Matt Kennard and Claire Provost, "Inside Lavasa, India's First Entirely Private City Built from Scratch," *Guardian*, November 19, 2015; Valeria Saiu, "The Three Pitfalls of Sustainable City: A Conceptual Framework for Evaluating the Theory-Practice Gap," *Sustainability* 9, no. 12 (2017).

17. Rina Chandran, "India Evicting 30 People an Hour as Cities Modernize— Activists," *Reuters*, February 23, 2018.

18. Jaffe, "How Are Those Cities of the Future Coming Along?"

19. Irene Quaile, "Masdar Eco-City Rebounds after Setbacks," December 3, 2013, http://www.dw.com/en/masdar-eco-city-rebounds-after-setbacks/ a-16664316.

20. For one example: Ian James, "Songdo: No Man's City," *Korea Exposé*, October 14, 2016, https://www.koreaexpose.com/songdo-no-mans-city/.

21. Briony Harris, "A Smart City Is Being Built in Toronto," World Economic Forum, October 27, 2017, https://www.weforum.org/agenda/2017/10/ google-parent-alphabet-is-building-a-model-smart-city-district-but-will-people -want-to-live-there/; Sidewalk Toronto, "New District in Toronto Will Tackle the Challenges of Urban Growth."

22. Laura Bliss, "Toronto's 'Smart City' Could Be a Blueprint for Developers," *CityLab* (blog), January 9, 2018, https://www.citylab.com/design/2018/01/ when-a-tech-giant-plays-waterfront-developer/549590/.

23. Jason Plautz, "Sidewalk Labs Advisor Quits Toronto Project over Privacy Concerns," *Smart Cities Dive* (blog), October 8, 2018, https://www .smartcitiesdive.com/news/sidewalk-labs-advisor-quits-toronto-project-over -privacy-concerns/539034/.

24. Ari-Veikko Anttiroiko, "U-Cities Reshaping Our Future: Reflections on Ubiquitous Infrastructure as an Enabler of Smart Urban Development," *AI and Society*, February 2013.

25. IHS Online Newsroom, "Smart Cities to Rise Fourfold in Number from 2013 to 2025," *IHS Markit* (blog), July 29, 2014, http://news.ihsmarkit .com/press-release/design-supply-chain-media/smart-cities-rise-fourfold -number-2013-2025.

26. Shelton, Zook, and Wiig, "The 'Actually Existing Smart City.'"

27. Jason Deign, "Retrofitting Smart Cities," *The Network: Cisco's Technology News Site* (blog), September 17, 2014, https://newsroom.cisco.com/feature -content?type=webcontent&articleId=1489176.

28. EPIC, "'Smart City in a Box,'" EU Platform for Intelligent Cities, accessed April 9, 2018, http://www.epic-cities.eu/content/smart-city-box; Greg Lindsay, "IBM Offers Cash-Strapped Mayors a Smarter City-in-a-Box," *Fast Company*, June 6, 2011; Microsoft, Singapore News Center, "Surbana Jurong and Microsoft Develop Cloud-Based Smart City in a Box Solutions, Enhance App Offerings," November 25, 2016, https://news.microsoft.com/en-sg/2016/11/25/surbana-jurong-and-microsoft-develop-cloud-based-smart-city-in-a-box-solutions-enhance-app-offerings/.

29. Lindsay, "IBM Offers Cash-Strapped Mayors a Smarter City-in-a-Box."

30. Microsoft, Singapore News Center, "Surbana Jurong and Microsoft Develop Cloud-Based Smart City in a Box Solutions, Enhance App Offerings."

31. Cisco and Smart Cities Council, "Smart City Readiness," 2014; Smart Cities Council, "Smart City Readiness Guide: The Planning Manual for Building Tomorrow's Cities Today," 2017, https://readinessguide.smartcitiescouncil.com/.

32. Tod Newcombe, "Santander: The Smartest Smart City," *Governing*, May 2014, http://www.governing.com/topics/urban/gov-santander-spain-smart-city.html.

33. Lyndsay Winkley, "San Diego Police to Continue Using Gunshot Detection System, despite Some Criticism," *San Diego Union-Tribune*, October 7, 2017.

34. Nanette Byrnes, "Cities Find Rewards in Cheap Technologies," *MIT Technology Review*, February 2015.

35. Ross Tieman, "Barcelona: Smart City Revolution in Progress," *Financial Times*, October 25, 2017.

36. Felipe Gil-Castineira, Enrique Costa-Montenegro, Francisco Gonzalez-Castano, Cristina Lopez-Bravo, Timo Ojala, and Raja Bose, "Experiences inside the Ubiquitous Oulu Smart City," *Computer* 44, no. 6 (June 2011): 48–55; Annelies van der Stoep, "City-Zen: Virtual Power Plant," Amsterdam Smart City, accessed October 29, 2018, https://amsterdamsmartcity.com/projects/city-zen-virtual-power-plant.

37. Robert Mitchum, "Chicago Becomes First City to Launch Array of Things," *UChicago News*, August 29, 2016, https://news.uchicago.edu/article/2016/08/29/chicago-becomes-first-city-launch-array-things.

38. Denise Linn, "Documentation from the Array of Things Public Meeting at Association House of Chicago," Smart Chicago, November 9, 2017, http://www.smartchicagocollaborative.org/documentation-from-the-array-of-things-public-meeting-at-association-house-of-chicago/.

39. Sean Thornton, "A Guide to Chicago's Array of Things Initiative," Data-Smart City Solutions, January 2, 2018, https://datasmart.ash.harvard.edu/news/article/a-guide-to-chicagos-array-of-things-initiative-1190.

40. Laura Forlano, "Decentering the Human in the Design of Collaborative Cities," *Design Issues* 32, no. 3 (Summer 2016).

41. Smart City Expo World Congress, "Empower Cities, Empower People Report 2017," 63.

42. Katharine S. Willis and Alessandro Aurigi, *Digital and Smart Cities* (New York: Routledge, 2018).

43. Carlo Ratti and Anthony Townsend, "The Social Nexus," *Scientific American* 305, no. 3 (2011): 42–49.

44. Marcus Foth, Laura Forlano, Christine Satchell, and Martin Gibbs, eds., *From Social Butterfly to Engaged Citizen: Urban Informatics, Social Media, Ubiquitous Computing, and Mobile Technology to Support Citizen Engagement* (Cambridge, MA: MIT Press, 2011); Marcus Foth, Martin Brynskov, and Timo Ojala, *Citizen's Right to the Digital City: Urban Interfaces, Activism, and Placemaking* (Berlin: Springer, 2015); Michiel de Lange and Martijn de Waal, "Owning the City: New Media and Citizen Engagement in Urban Design," *First Monday* 18, no. 11 (2013); Peter van Waart and Ingrid Mulder, "Meaningful Interactions in a Smart City," in *Distributed, Ambient, and Pervasive Interactions*, ed. Norbert Streitz and Panos Markopoulos (Cham, Switzerland: Springer International, 2014), 617–628; Robert G. Hollands, "Critical Interventions into the Corporate Smart City," *Cambridge Journal of Regions, Economy and Society* 8, no. 1 (March 1, 2015): 61–77; Usman Haque, "Surely There's a Smarter Approach to Smart Cities?," *Wired UK*, April 17, 2012.

45. Lange and Waal, "Owning the City."

46. Scott McQuire, "Rethinking Media Events: Large Screens, Public Space Broadcasting and Beyond," *New Media and Society* 12, no. 4 (2010): 567–582.

47. Vic Vela, "Meet Brian Corrigan, Denver's 'Oh Heck Yeah' Phenom," *Confluence Denver*, July 24, 2013. http://www.confluence-denver.com/features/corrigan_072431.aspx.

48. Nathan Heffel, "Denver Street Arcade Attracts Gamers of All Ages," *Morning Edition*, NPR, June 30, 2014.

49. J. D. Ross, "ISchool, AT&T, City of Syracuse Partner to Launch Civic Data Hackathon Focused on Snow Removal," *SU News* (blog), February 9, 2018, https://news.syr.edu/blog/2018/02/09/ischool-att-city-of-syracuse-partner-to-launch-civic-data-hackathon-focused-on-snow-removal/.

50. Saskia Sassen, "Open Sourcing the Neighborhood," *Forbes*, November 10, 2013.

51. Alicia Rouault, "A Bottom-Up Smart City?," *Data-Smart City Solutions* (blog), December 20, 2013, https://datasmart.ash.harvard.edu/news/article/a-bottom-up-smart-city-355.

52. Berst, "How to Guarantee a Win from the Smart Cities Council Readiness Challenge Grants."

53. "Cisco Announces \$1 Billion Program for Smart Cities," *The Network: Cisco's Technology News Site* (blog), November 14, 2017, https://newsroom.cisco.com/press-release-content?type=webcontent&articleId=1895705.

54. Roy, "The Smart City Paradigm in India."

55. Cisco and Smart Cities Council, "Smart City Readiness," 2014.

56. Roy, "The Smart City Paradigm in India."

57. Esther Somers, "City-Zen: Retrofitting Homes," Amsterdam Smart City, accessed October 29, 2018, https://amsterdamsmartcity.com/projects/city-zen-retrofitting.

58. IHS Online Newsroom, "Smart Cities to Rise Fourfold in Number from 2013 to 2025."

59. Roy, "The Smart City Paradigm in India."

60. Herman van den Bosch, "Smart Cities 1.0, 2.0, 3.0. What's Next?," July 4, 2017, http://smartcityhub.com/collaborative-city/smart-cities-1-0-2-0-3-0-whats-next/.

61. Nicole DuPuis and Elias Stahl, "Trends in Smart City Development," National League of Cities, 2016.

**Chapter 3**

1. Pethuru Raj and Anupama C. Raman, *Intelligent Cities: Enabling Tools and Technology* (Boca Raton, FL: CRC Press, 2015).

2. "Microsoft CityNext: Technology Solutions for Smart Cities," accessed April 11, 2018, https://enterprise.microsoft.com/en-us/industries/citynext/.

3. Mark Weiser, "The Computer for the 21st Century," *Scientific American*, September 1991.

4. Mark Weiser, "Open House," *ITP Review*, March 1996, http://www.itp.tsoa.nyu.edu/~review/.

5. Paul Dourish and Genevieve Bell, *Divining a Digital Future: Mess and Mythology in Ubiquitous Computing* (Cambridge, MA: MIT Press, 2011).

6. City of Vienna, "Smart City Wien Strategy and Objectives," accessed October 26, 2018, https://smartcity.wien.gv.at/site/en/the-initiative/strategy-objectives/.

7. World Bank, "Starting an Open Data Initiative," October 24, 2013.

8. Emily DeVoe, "Instagram Helps Mobile Identify 1,256 Blighted Properties," *WKRG News 5*, November 20, 2015, http://wkrg.com/2015/11/20/instagram-helps-mobile-identify-1256-blighted-properties/.

9. Neal Ungerleider, "Waze Is Driving into City Hall," *Fast Company*, April 15, 2015.

10. Siemens, *Ingenuity for Life Creates Perfect Places*, 2017, https://www.youtube.com/watch?v=mFXUm6mj4Xc.

11. Myron W. Krueger, "Responsive Environments," in *Proceedings of the June 13–16, 1977, National Computer Conference, AFIPS '77* (New York: ACM, 1977), 423–433.

12. For one example, see Microsoft Azure, *Microsoft IoT for Smart Buildings*, 2017. https://www.youtube.com/watch?time_continue=23&v=d55rBuB9D7s.

13. Low Teck Seng, "IoT as a Key Enabler to Singapore's Smart Nation Vision," *IEEE Internet of Things* (blog), March 14, 2018, https://iot.ieee.org/conferences-events/wf-iot-2014-videos/47-newsletter/march-2018.html.

14. Elizabeth Montalbano, "Smart-City Technology Harvests Energy From Footsteps," *Design News* 68, no. 6 (June 2013): 30–31.

15. A. Zanella, N. Bui, A. Castellani, L. Vangelista, and M. Zorzi, "Internet of Things for Smart Cities," *IEEE Internet of Things Journal* 1, no. 1 (February 2014): 22–32.

16. V. Zdraveski, K. Mishev, D. Trajanov, and L. Kocarev, "ISO-Standardized Smart City Platform Architecture and Dashboard," *IEEE Pervasive Computing* 16, no. 2 (April 2017): 35–43; Rob Kitchin, Tracey P. Lauriault, and Gavin McArdle, "Knowing and Governing Cities through Urban Indicators, City Benchmarking and Real-Time Dashboards," *Regional Studies, Regional Science* 2, no. 1 (January 1, 2015): 6–28.

17. Kitchin, Lauriault, and McArdle, "Knowing and Governing Cities through Urban Indicators, City Benchmarking and Real-Time Dashboards."

18. Felipe Gil-Castineira, Enrique Costa-Montenegro, Francisco Gonzalez-Castano, Cristina Lopez-Bravo, Timo Ojala, and Raja Bose, "Experiences inside the Ubiquitous Oulu Smart City," *Computer* 44, no. 6 (June 2011): 48–55.

19. Michael Batty, "Deconstructing Smart Cities," in *Technologies for Urban and Spatial Planning: Virtual Cities and Territories*, ed. Nuno Norte Pinto, Jose Antonio Tenedorio, Antonio Pais Antunes, and Josep Roca Cladera (Hershey, PA: IGI Global, 2014).

20. Lynn Horsley, "KC Installs First of 25 Smart City Kiosks Downtown," *Kansas City Star*, March 7, 2016.

21.  Steve Strunsky, "Digital Kiosks to Link Newark People to Each Other and the Internet," *NJ.com*, October 17, 2016, http://www.nj.com/essex/index.ssf/2016/10/digital_kiosks_to_link_newark_people_to_the_city_a.html.

22.  L. G. Pee, A. Kankanhalli, and V. C. Y. On Show, "Bridging the Digital Divide: Use of Public Internet Kiosks in Mauritius," *Journal of Global Information Management* 18, no. 1 (2010).

23.  City of Stockholm, "How the Smart City Develops," accessed October 28, 2018, https://international.stockholm.se/governance/smart-and-connected-city/how-the-smart-city-develops/.

24.  US Department of Transportation, "U.S. Department of Transportation Announces Columbus as Winner of Unprecedented $40 Million Smart City Challenge," *Department of Transportation* (blog), June 23, 2016. https://www.transportation.gov/briefing-room/us-department-transportation-announces-columbus-winner-unprecedented-40-million-smart.

25.  Chris Nelson, "Masdar City's Driverless Cars System Celebrates Milestone," *National*, November 30, 2016, http://www.thenational.ae/business/technology/masdar-citys-driverless-cars-system-celebrates-milestone.

26.  Erica E. Phillips, "When Robots Take to the Sidewalks," *Wall Street Journal*, April 17, 2017.

27.  Ibid.

28.  Ross Tieman, "Barcelona: Smart City Revolution in Progress," *Financial Times*, October 25, 2017.

29.  Sarah Brayne, "Big Data Surveillance: The Case of Policing," *American Sociological Review* 82, no. 5 (August 2017).

30.  Safiya Umoja Noble, *Algorithms of Oppression: How Search Engines Reinforce Racism* (New York: NYU Press, 2018); Virginia Eubanks, *Automating Inequality: How High-Tech Tools Profile, Police, and Punish the Poor* (New York: St. Martin's Press, 2018); Tarleton Gillespie, "The Politics of 'Platforms,'" *New Media and Society* 12, no. 3 (May 1, 2010): 347–364.

31.  Mike Ananny and Kate Crawford, "Seeing without Knowing: Limitations of the Transparency Ideal and Its Application to Algorithmic Accountability," *New Media and Society*, December 13, 2016; John C. Bertot, Paul T. Jaeger, and Justin M. Grimes, "Using ICTs to Create a Culture of Transparency: E-Government and Social Media as Openness and Anti-Corruption Tools for Societies," *Government Information Quarterly* 27, no. 3 (July 1, 2010): 264–271.

32. Rahm Emanuel, "Open Data Executive Order (No. 2012-2)," City of Chicago, 2012, https://www.cityofchicago.org/city/en/narr/foia/open_data_executiveorder.html.

33. Linda Rosencrance, "In Chicago, Smart City Data Drives Innovation, Efficiency," *IoT Agenda*, May 2017. https://internetofthingsagenda.techtarget.com/feature/In-Chicago-smart-city-data-drives-innovation-efficiency.

34. Natasha Korecki, "Battle-Scarred Rahm Stares down Toughest Election Ever," *Politico*, April 24, 2018, https://www.politico.com/story/2018/04/24/rahm-emanuel-faces-toughest-reelection-yet-547834.

35. Keller Easterling, *Extrastatecraft: The Power of Infrastructure Space* (London: Verso, 2014), 17.

36. O. Halpern, J. LeCavalier, N. Calvillo, and W. Pietsch, "Test-Bed Urbanism," *Public Culture* 25 (2013): 292.

37. William H Whyte, *The Social Life of Small Urban Spaces* (New York: Project for Public Spaces, 1980).

38. Germaine Halegoua, "The Policy and Export of Ubiquitous Place: Investigating South Korean U-Cities," in *From Social Butterfly to Engaged Citizen: Urban Informatics, Social Media, Ubiquitous Computing, and Mobile Technology to Support Citizen Engagement*, ed. Marcus Foth, Laura Forlano, Christine Satchell, and Martin Gibbs (Cambridge, MA: MIT Press, 2011), 315–334.

**Chapter 4**

1. Robert G. Hollands, "Will the Real Smart City Please Stand Up?," *City* 12, no. 3 (2008): 303–320; Adam Greenfield, *Against the Smart City*, 1.3 edition (Do projects, 2013); Michael Batty, "How Disruptive Is the Smart Cities Movement?," *Environment and Planning B: Planning and Design* 43, no. 3 (May 1, 2016): 441–443; Souvanic Roy, "The Smart City Paradigm in India: Issues and Challenges of Sustainability and Inclusiveness," *Social Scientist* 44, no. 5/6 (2016): 29–48; Rob Kitchin, "The Real-Time City? Big Data and Smart Urbanism," *GeoJournal* 79, no. 1 (2014): 1–14.

2. Jane Jacobs, *The Death and Life of Great American Cities* (New York: Vintage, 1961); Lewis Mumford, *The Culture of Cities* (New York: Harcourt, Brace, 1938).

3. Dan Hill, "Essay: On the Smart City; Or, a 'Manifesto' for Smart Citizens Instead," *cityofsound*, February 2013, http://www.cityofsound.com/blog/2013/02/on-the-smart-city-a-call-for-smart-citizens-instead.html.

4. Cisco and Smart Cities Council, "Smart City Readiness," 2014.

5. Jason Deign, "Retrofitting Smart Cities," *The Network: Cisco's Technology News Site* (blog), September 17, 2014, https://newsroom.cisco.com/feature-content?type=webcontent&articleId=1489176.

6. Jane Wakefield, "Tomorrow's Cities: Do You Want to Live in a Smart City?," *BBC News*, August 19, 2013.

7. Anna Kordunsky, "Overcoming the Sustainability Challenge: An Interview with Guruduth Banavar," *Journal of International Affairs* 65, no. 2 (Spring/Summer 2012): 149.

8. Ibid., 150.

9. See Germaine R. Halegoua, *The Digital City: Media and the Social Production of Place* (New York: NYU Press, 2019).

10. Ibid.

11. Greenfield, *Against the Smart City*.

12. Catherine Mulligan, "Citizen Engagement in Smart Cities," in *Smart Citizens*, ed. Drew Hemment and Anthony Townsend (Manchester, UK: FutureEverything Publications, 2013), 83.

13. Matthew Cotton and Patrick Devine-Wright, "Making Electricity Networks 'Visible': Industry Actor Representations of 'Publics' and Public Engagement in Infrastructure Planning," *Public Understanding of Science* 21, no. 1 (January 1, 2012): 17–35; Sanda Kaufman and Kevin Snape, "Public Attitudes toward Urban Infrastructure: The Northeast Ohio Experience," *Public Works Management and Policy* 1, no. 3 (January 1997): 224–244.

14. Anthony McLean, Harriet Bulkeley, and Mike Crang, "Negotiating the Urban Smart Grid: Socio-Technical Experimentation in the City of Austin," *Urban Studies* 53, no. 15 (November 1, 2016): 3246–3263.

15. Dorien Zandbergen, "'We Are Sensemakers': The (Anti-)Politics of Smart City Co-Creation," *Public Culture* 29, no. 3 (September 2017): 539–562.

16. For further description and analysis of the exclusivity of smart city events, see Halegoua, *The Digital City*; and Germaine Halegoua, "Class Distinctions in Urban Broadband Initiatives," in *The Routledge Companion to Media and Class*, ed. Erika Polson, Lynn Schofield Clark, and Radhika Gajjala (London: Routledge, 2019).

17. Smart City Expo World Congress, "Empower Cities, Empower People Report 2017," 63.

18. US Department of Transportation, "Smart City Challenge," September 28, 2016, https://www.transportation.gov/smartcity.

19. Dietmar Offenhuber, *Waste Is Information: Infrastructure Legibility and Governance* (Cambridge, MA: MIT Press, 2017), 206.

20. Kate Crawford, "Following You: Disciplines of Listening in Social Media," *Continuum: Journal of Media and Cultural Studies* 23, no. 4 (2009).

21. City of New York, Mayor's Office of Media and Entertainment, "Road Map for the Digital City: Achieving New York City's Digital Future," Spring 2011.

22. Bonnie J. Johnson and Germaine R. Halegoua, "Potential and Challenges for Social Media in the Neighborhood Context," *Journal of Urban Technology* 21, no. 4 (October 2, 2014): 51–75.

23. City of New York, "Road Map for the Digital City," 29.

24. Nikki Goth Itoi, "Oracle Voice: New Ways to Embrace the Power of the Crowd," *Forbes*, November 20, 2014.

25. Eric Gordon and Gabriel Mugar, "Civic Media Practice: Identification and Evaluation of Media and Technology That Facilitates Democratic Process," Engagement Lab at Emerson College, Boston, 2018.

26. London City Hall, "Civic Crowdfunding Programme," June 16, 2016, https://www.london.gov.uk//what-we-do/business-and-economy/supporting-londons-sectors/smart-london/civic-crowdfunding-programme.

27. Tara Deschamps, "Sidewalk Labs Advisory Panel Member Saadia Muzaffar Quits, Citing 'Deep Dismay,'" *Financial Post*, October 5, 2018.

28. Sarah Brayne, "Big Data Surveillance: The Case of Policing," *American Sociological Review* 82, no. 5 (August 2017); Safiya Umoja Noble, *Algorithms of Oppression: How Search Engines Reinforce Racism* (New York: NYU Press, 2018); Virginia Eubanks, *Automating Inequality: How High-Tech Tools Profile, Police, and Punish the Poor* (New York: St. Martin's Press, 2018).

29. Hill, "Essay."

30. Mulligan, "Citizen Engagement in Smart Cities," 83–86.

31. Dan Hill, "Smart Citizens Make Smart Cities," in Hemment and Townsend, *Smart Citizens*, 87–90.

32. Greenfield, *Against the Smart City*.

33. Hill, "Essay"; Frank Kresin, "A Manifesto for Smart Citizens," in Hemment and Townsend, *Smart Citizens*, 91–94; "Smart Citizens," FutureEverything, 2013, http://futureeverything.org/wp-content/uploads/2014/03/smartcitizens1.pdf; Carlo Ratti and Anthony Townsend, "Harnessing Residents' Electronic Devices Will Yield Truly Smart Cities," *Scientific American*, September 2011.

34. Beth Simone Noveck, "Re-imagining Government through Civic Media: Three Pathways to Institutional Innovation," in *Civic Media*, ed. Eric Gordon and Paul Mihailidis (Cambridge, MA: MIT Press, 2016).

35. Nick Couldry and Alison Powell, "Big Data from the Bottom Up," *Big Data and Society* 1, no. 2 (July 2014).

36. Rob Kitchin, Tracey P. Lauriault, and Gavin McArdle, "Knowing and Governing Cities through Urban Indicators, City Benchmarking and Real-Time Dashboards," *Regional Studies, Regional Science* 2, no. 1 (January 1, 2015): 6–28; Ruth Beilin and Ashlea Hunter, "Co-Constructing the Sustainable City:

How Indicators Help Us 'Grow' More than Just Food in Community Gardens," *Local Environment* 16, no. 6 (July 2011): 523–538.

37. Joke Van Assche, Thomas Block, and Herwig Reynaert, "Can Community Indicators Live Up to Their Expectations? The Case of the Flemish City Monitor for Liveable and Sustainable Urban Development," *Applied Research in Quality of Life* 5, no. 4 (2010): 341–352.

38. Sarah Williams, "Big Data for a Public Good," re:publica, accessed October 12, 2018, https://www.youtube.com/watch?v=cHy__jxA1Ys.

39. "BreatheLife," *Purpose*, accessed November 15, 2018, https://www.purpose.com/case_studies/breathelife/.

40. *Digital Matatus*, accessed November 2, 2018, http://www.digitalmatatus.com/about.html.

41. "Digital Stewards Training," *Allied Media Projects*, March 13, 2015, https://alliedmedia.org/dctp/digitalstewards.

42. Amy Crawford, "Detroit Imagines a Citizen-Led Smart City," *CityLab* (blog), May 31, 2017, https://www.citylab.com/life/2017/05/detroit-imagines-a-citizen-led-smart-city/528441/.

43. Alessandra Orofino, *It's Our City. Let's Fix It*, 2014, https://www.ted.com/talks/alessandra_orofino_it_s_our_city_let_s_fix_it?language=en; Ruth Pearce, "Meu Rio," *CDJ Plus* (blog), July 28, 2017, http://www.oxfordjournals.org/cdjc/tag/meu-rio/.

44. For further analysis, see Halegoua, *The Digital City*; and Germaine Halegoua, "The Policy and Export of Ubiquitous Place: Investigating South Korean U-Cities," in *From Social Butterfly to Engaged Citizen: Urban Informatics, Social Media, Ubiquitous Computing, and Mobile Technology to Support Citizen Engagement*, ed. Marcus Foth, Laura Forlano, Christine Satchell, and Martin Gibbs (Cambridge, MA: MIT Press, 2011), 315–334.

### Chapter 5

1. Laura Bliss, "Toronto's 'Smart City' Could Be a Blueprint for Developers," *CityLab* (blog), January 9, 2018, https://www.citylab.com/design/2018/01/when-a-tech-giant-plays-waterfront-developer/549590/.

2. Stephen Goldsmith and Susan Crawford, *The Responsive City: Engaging Communities through Data-Smart Governance* (San Francisco: John Wiley and Sons, 2014).

3. Taylor Shelton, Matthew Zook, and Alan Wiig, "The 'Actually Existing Smart City,'" *Cambridge Journal of Regions, Economy and Society* 8, no. 1 (March 1, 2015): 13–25.

4. Catherine D'Ignazio and Lauren Klein, "Feminist Data Visualization," in *Proceedings from the Workshop on Visualization for the Digital Humanities*, 2016.

5. Isabel Dyck, "Feminist Geography, the 'Everyday,' and Local-Global Relations: Hidden Spaces of Place-Making," *Canadian Geographer* 49, no. 3 (September 2005): 233–243.

6. Megan Heim LaFrombois, "Blind Spots and Pop-up Spots: A Feminist Exploration into the Discourses of Do-It-Yourself (DIY) Urbanism," *Urban Studies* 54, no. 2 (February 1, 2017): 421–436; Leslie Kern and Gerda Wekerle, "Gendered Spaces of Redevelopment: Gendered Politics of City Building," *Research in Urban Sociology* 9 (February 2008): 233–262.

7. For example, Dan Hill, "Essay: On the Smart City; Or, a 'Manifesto' for Smart Citizens Instead," *cityofsound*, February 2013, http://www.cityofsound .com/blog/2013/02/on-the-smart-city-a-call-for-smart-citizens-instead.html; "Smart Citizens," FutureEverything, 2013, http://futureeverything.org/wp -content/uploads/2014/03/smartcitizens1.pdf; Thomas Ermacora and Lucy Bullivant, *Recoded City: Co-creating Urban Futures* (London: Routledge, 2016).

# ADDITIONAL RESOURCES

**Smart Cities**

Cardullo, Paolo, Cesare di Feliciantonio, and Rob Kitchin, eds. *The Right to the Smart City*. Bingley, UK: Emerald Publishing, 2019.

Goldsmith, Stephen, and Susan Crawford. *The Responsive City: Engaging Communities through Data-Smart Governance*. San Francisco: Jossey-Bass, 2014.

Green, Ben. *The Smart Enough City: Putting Technology in Its Place to Reclaim Our Urban Future*. Cambridge, MA: MIT Press, 2019.

Greenfield, Adam. *Against the Smart City*. 1.3 edition. Do projects, 2013.

Hemment, Drew, and Anthony Townsend, eds. *Smart Citizens*. Manchester, UK: FutureEverything Publications, 2013.

Marvin, Simon, Andrés Luque-Ayala, and Colin McFarlane, eds. *Smart Urbanism: Utopian Vision or False Dawn?* New York: Routledge, 2016.

Picon, Antoine. *Smart Cities: A Spatialised Intelligence*. West Sussex, UK: John Wiley & Sons, 2015.

Shepard, Mark, ed. *Sentient City: Ubiquitous Computing, Architecture, and the Future of Urban Space*. Cambridge, MA: MIT Press, 2011.

Townsend, Anthony M. *Smart Cities: Big Data, Civic Hackers, and the Quest for a New Utopia*. New York: W. W. Norton, 2013.

Willis, Katharine S., and Alessandro Aurigi. *Digital and Smart Cities*. New York: Routledge, 2018.


**Related Work**

Eubanks, Virginia. *Automating Inequality: How High-Tech Tools Profile, Police, and Punish the Poor*. New York: St. Martin's Press, 2018.

Foth, Marcus, Laura Forlano, Martin Gibbs, and Christine Satchell, eds. *From Social Butterfly to Engaged Citizen: Urban Informatics, Social Media, Ubiquitous*

*Computing, and Mobile Technology to Support Citizen Engagement*. Cambridge, MA: MIT Press, 2011.

Gordon, Eric, and Paul Mihailidis, eds. *Civic Media: Technology, Design, Practice*. Cambridge, MA: MIT Press, 2016.

Mattern, Shannon. *Code and Clay, Data and Dirt*. Minneapolis: University of Minnesota Press, 2017.

McLaren, Duncan, and Julian Agyeman. *Sharing Cities: A Case for Truly Smart and Sustainable Cities*. Cambridge, MA: MIT Press, 2015.

**Resources**

AI Now Institute https://ainowinstitute.org/

Allied Media Projects https://www.alliedmedia.org/

Data & Society https://datasociety.net/

Data For Black Lives http://d4bl.org/

Data Justice Lab https://datajusticelab.org/

Media Justice Network https://mediajustice.org/

Sentient City Survival Kit http://survival.sentientcity.net/

Smart Cities for All https://smartcities4all.org/

Sunlight Foundation https://sunlightfoundation.com/

# INDEX

Note: Figures are indicated by "f" following page numbers.

**The MIT Press Essential Knowledge Series**